BRIGHTON & HOVE ALBION

Miscellany

Paul Camillin

Brighton & Hove Albion Miscellany

© Paul Camillin

The author has asserted his rights in accordance with the *Copyright, Designs and Patents Act* 1988 to be identified as the author of this work.

Published by:
Pavilion Publishing (Brighton) Ltd
Richmond House
Richmond Road
Brighton BN2 3RL
Tel: 01273 623222
Fax: 01273 625526
Email: info@pavpub.com
Web: www.pavpub.com

First published 2006

A Catalogue record for this book is available from the British Library.

ISBN-13: 978 1 84196 188 0
ISBN-10: 1 84196 188 4

Editor: Grace Fairley (www.thebigwideword.com)
Cover design and page layout: Tony Pitt
Printing: Patterson Printing Ltd (Tunbridge Wells)

E-147-07-06

Foreword

by Peter Ward

Within the pages of this book are a set of wonderful tales and trivia from the history of our great club. Many from the heady days of the 1970s, a time which will be forever etched on my memory. There are also quirky stats, stories and anecdotes from other eras, highs and lows which capture the eye.

All the club's great characters are represented. From the late 1970s and early 1980s it features the likes of Alan Mullery, a fantastic manager, my great strike partner Spider Mellor, our never-say-die skipper Brian Horton and the class act that was Mark Lawrenson. Great friendships were forged. Gary Williams, Andy Rollings, Chris Cattlin, Steve Foster, Steve Piper, Grease (if you don't know who Grease is, you'll find out that's what we called Gary Stevens in those days)... the list goes on and on.

There are also all the great and glorious names from the past: Charlie Webb, Tommy Cook, Denis Foreman, Glen Wilson – a great servant to the Seagulls, and our sponge man for those glory days. And there are those who we have seen serve the club so well in the modern era: Garry Nelson, Charlie Oatway, Micky Adams, Dick Knight and Bobby Zamora – a player who I loved watching play for Albion, and one I would have loved to have played alongside.

I did play alongside some great characters in what I regard as our club's most glorious period in its long and colourful history. They were fantastic days to be a player at Brighton, and the bond between us and the fans was so strong. It even remains today, so much that whenever I am in Brighton and Hove I always get a fantastic welcome from you all. I hope you enjoy reading this book as much as I did. And keep on supporting our great club as it makes more tales for future generations.

Acknowledgements

Thanks to: Chris, Grace, Joanna and Tanis at Pavilion Publishing – together they have worked wonders to get this book published in such a short space of time; Peter Ward for writing the foreword; to those Albion legends whose kind words adorn the back cover; John Vinicombe and the late Roger Harris, whose epic history books on the Albion proved invaluable when it came to research; Roy Chuter and Tim Dudding, both very good friends and excellent suppliers of inspiration and support; and John Baine for giving permission to use his brilliant Goldstone Ghosts poem and hilarious We Want Falmer lyrics. Finally, massive thanks to Albion historian Tim Carder who co-wrote *Seagulls* and the *Albion A-Z* with Roger Harris. Tim's excellent website www.albionhistory.org.uk also proved invaluable. In addition, I would like to thank Tim, not just for providing, verifying and checking many of the facts within the book, but for all the unpaid hours he puts in for the football club so many of us love. The phrase 'unsung hero' is often overused, but for Tim I use it in the truest sense of the phrase: on behalf of all Albion fans, you are a real Albion legend.

Introduction

Brighton & Hove Albion Miscellany is a collection of interesting trivia, quirky facts and fascinating anecdotes from the long and colourful history of Brighton & Hove Albion Football Club. The book follows no set order – there are no chapters or sections, it is simply a collection of entries. Each different entry is entirely random, and only the entries relating to Albion's five championships (1910, 1958, 1965, 2001 and 2002) Champions I-V run in any sort of chronological order. Within these pages you will find entries relating to some of the club's finest players, legendary characters, most-famous victories and glorious days since the conception of the Albion in 1901. There are also some tales from the Albion's darker days and stories concerning the less well-known or successful players to wear the blue and white of Albion. It's a book that I hope will promote debates and discussions about the Albion, at home, in the pub, at the match... I hope that you enjoy reading it as much as I enjoyed writing it.

Paul Camillin
August 2006

Abbreviations

1R . . . . *First round*

1RR . . . . *First round replay*

A . . . . *Goals against*

Aet . . . . *After extra time*

Apps . . . . *Appearances*

AMC . . . . *Associate Members' Cup*

D . . . . *Games drawn*

F . . . . *Goals for*

FC . . . . *Football Club*

FAC . . . . *FA Cup*

GD . . . . *Goal difference*

Gls . . . . *Goals*

FA . . . . *Football Association*

L . . . . *Games lost*

LC . . . . *League Cup*

P . . . . *Games played*

Pts . . . . *Points*

QF . . . . *Quarter-final*

SF . . . . *Semi-final*

W . . . . *Games won*

Albion's conception

The exact date of Brighton & Hove Albion Football Club's birth has been a source of debate for the past century, but it is now virtually certain that the club was formed on 24 June 1901. For many years, however, it was documented in several soccer history books that Brighton & Hove Albion originally formed in 1900 as Brighton & Hove Rangers, and that when the club turned professional, they simply changed the suffix from Rangers to Albion. Even as recently as 1979, in his book *Up, Up And Away*, much-respected *Argus* reporter John Vinicombe wrote about '79 years of history', which would of course mean Albion came into being in 1900. The tireless efforts of club historian Tim Carder and the late Roger Harris unearthed a very different story, which they published in the incredible tome *Seagulls! The Story Of Brighton & Hove Albion FC* in 1993. The book revealed for the first time the true date and story of Albion's birth. It concluded that Brighton & Hove Rangers had disbanded in 1901 and described how, in the wake of the collapse of Rangers, Brighton & Hove Albion were formed at the Seven Stars public house on Ship Street (now an O'Neill's pub) on 24 June 1901. Quite why the Albion suffix was adopted remains open to debate. Some historians believe Albion's founder and first ever manager John Jackson had close links with West Bromwich Albion. Carder and Harris's book disputes this, though; their research couldn't link Jackson to West Brom. Instead, they suggest 'Albion' was probably used because it was a popular name with a number of commercial enterprises in Brighton and Hove at the time. Around the turn of the century, you could book a room at the Royal Albion Hotel or, if you fancied something stronger, sup a pint, brewed by the Albion Brewery, at the Albion Inn, all establishments owned by prominent figures in the early days of the club. In 2006, the Albion name lives on in Brighton businesses. You can mortgage your house with the Albion Mortgage Company, book a cab with Albion Taxis or wolf down a doner kebab with chilli sauce or chicken kofte and chips prepared by Albion Kebabs – all businesses influenced by the football club, rather than the other way around.

Peruvians perused but not used

In 2005, Argentine forward Federico Turienzo became the first South American to play for Albion, but had events gone differently 26 years earlier, the honour could have gone to one of two Peruvians. The Albion were pushing for promotion to Division One when Percy Rojas and Juan-Carlos Oblitas, both of whom had been part of Peru's World Cup squad in the 1978 finals, arrived in Hove for trials in February 1979, with a view to a possible £400,000 joint transfer. The pair played in a secret, behind-closed-doors training match against Alec Stock's Bournemouth at Hove Greyhound Stadium. Manager Alan Mullery gleaned little from the exercise – he really needed to see the pair in competitive action – and with the added problems of registrations, the work permits required and the inevitable problems with the language barrier (neither player spoke good English), Mullery had severe doubts about the deal. He also had doubts about the age of Oblitas, who claimed to be 27, and in whom Mullery had the greater interest. Nonetheless, the club looked into the possibility of Oblitas signing for American side Tampa Bay Rowdies and being loaned out to Albion, but nothing came of it and the Peruvians eventually returned home.

Albion's first match

On 7 September 1901, the club played a friendly match against Shoreham on Dyke Road Field. Albion won 2-0 with goals from Clem Barker and Frank McAvoy. Albion's first competitive match was against Brighton Athletic on Saturday 21 September, when 1200 people attended an FA Cup preliminary round match at the club's then home ground, Sussex Cricket Club's County Ground. They had originally been drawn away in the competition but the two clubs agreed to switch the fixture. Albion won the match 6-2 and Bert Baker scored the club's first competitive goal on the way to a hat trick. The first league match came a week later on 28 September away to Shepherds Bush, where McAvoy and Barker were again on target in a 2-0 win, with the crowd also reported as 1200.

A great Cup run

In 1932/33, Albion enjoyed their then-best run in the FA Cup. The team kicked off in the qualifying rounds after an administrative error (see 'FA Cup records', page 53) but by the time they reached the 'proper' rounds they were firing on all cylinders and Albion won through to the third round of the competition, where they were drawn at home to First Division Chelsea. Goals from Arthur Attwood and Tug Wilson completed an historic 2-1 win, watched by 23,580. In round four, Albion knocked out Bradford Park Avenue and that set up a fifth-round home tie with West Ham United at the Goldstone. A huge crowd was expected and the local press offered the following advice:

> *Wear a cap if you can*
> *Get there soon*
> *Do your bit to pack*
> *Have the exact amount of admission money ready*

('Do your bit to pack' was a request to spectators standing on the terracing to ensure they left no gaps.) The match attracted a then-record crowd of 32,310 who saw Albion take a 2-0 lead through Reg Wilkinson and Arthur Attwood. The Hammers hit back to take the tie to a replay at Upton Park, where the Londoners won 1-0 after extra time.

Albion weren't Keane on Roy and Ian wasn't Wright either

Two of English football's biggest stars of the 1990s were linked with moves to the Albion before they made it big, but the club signed neither player. Via the same Irish link that had brought defender Paul McCarthy to the attention of the club, McCarthy's best friend and team-mate Roy Keane was recommended to Albion. According to Keane, writing in his biography, a trial was arranged but Albion felt Keane was too small to make it as a professional and contacted the Irishman the day before he was due to travel to Brighton to tell him the trial had been cancelled. Keane was devastated at the time, but eventually signed for Nottingham Forest and later moved to Old Trafford to become part of the hugely successful Manchester United team of the 1990s. He also captained the Irish national team. Ian

Wright, meanwhile, did get as far as a trial – he scored two goals in two reserve matches for Albion – and was expecting a contract offer from Chris Cattlin. The offer wasn't forthcoming, however, and Wright eventually signed professional forms with Crystal Palace. He later moved to Arsenal, where he became the club's all-time top goal scorer (although Thierry Henry has since surpassed his record) and was capped 31 times by England.

The move to the Goldstone Ground

In Albion's first season, 1901/02, the club used Sussex Cricket Club's County Ground to play their home matches, while amateurs Hove Football Club leased the Goldstone Ground from Alderman John Clark. On 22 February 1902, Albion were scheduled to play Southampton Wanderers in a friendly match, but with the County Ground already booked for an important Sussex Senior Cup semi-final fixture between Eastbourne and Shoreham, Albion were forced to find somewhere else to host the fixture and Hove agreed to let Albion use the Goldstone. Having won the match with Southampton 7-1, the same situation arose the following week, when Hailsham and Hove met in the second semi-final. Albion once again used the Goldstone to play their first competitive fixture on the ground that would eventually become their home for 95 years. Chesham Town were the opponents and Albion won 4-0. In the close season of 1902, Hove – with finances tight and £100 a year to pay for the rental of the Goldstone Ground – approached Albion to propose a ground-share between the clubs. Albion accepted and the two clubs continued the arrangement for two years, although the lower-ranked club's fixtures took precedence over Albion's matches, if they clashed with Hove's cup replays or rearranged fixtures. In 1904, Hove moved out and Albion became sole tenants.

Albion's foreign legion

A total of 37 foreigners had played for Albion by the end of the 2005/06 season. The first was George Moorhead, born in New Zealand (although he was of Irish nationality), who made just one appearance for Albion on 26 August 1922 in a goalless draw with Norwich City. Jack Dugnolle and Eric Lancelotte were both British citizens born in India. The first 100% foreigner was South African Denis Foreman, who arrived by steam boat via Southampton Docks and was signed by Billy Lane in March 1952, following a successful trial. He didn't play until the following October, when he appeared – and scored – in a 4-2 win over Aldershot at the Goldstone. Foreman went on to play 219 games for Albion and was also on the books of Sussex Cricket Club for 15 years. Wilf Smith was actually born Smit in Neumünster in Germany in 1946, but in the unforgiving post-war years his parents adopted the much more English name of Smith when they moved to Yorkshire, where Wilf was raised. There was an unsuccessful Israeli influx in the early 1980s and an Eastern European invasion in the late 1980s and early 1990s, with Sergei Gotsmanov, Igor Gurinovich and Stefan Iovan all arriving during Barry Lloyd's tenure as manager. Lloyd was unafraid of the foreign market, and often looked abroad for new faces. Seven foreigners made their debuts for the club while Lloyd was in charge, and in the early 1990s he constantly scoured the European market for cut-price foreign stars. He also brought back several English players from spells on the continent (Mike Small, John Byrne and Mark Farrington) and at one time he was linked with a move for Cameroon's 1990 World Cup captain Stephen Tataw. However, current boss Mark McGhee has been the most cosmopolitan of Albion managers and has given more debuts to foreigners than any other – nine in total, as at the end of the 2005/06 season.

Albion's foreign players

Player and date of Albion debut	Country of birth	Albion apps	Albion goals
George Moorhead* (26 August 1922)	New Zealand	1	0
Jack Dugnolle* (2 November 1935)	India	66	6
Eric Lancelotte* (6 March 1948)	India	62	15
Denis Foreman (25 October 1952)	South Africa	219	69
Eric Hodge (2 October 1957)	South Africa	4	0
Wilf Smith (16 October 1974)	Germany	5	0

continued

Albion's foreign players (continued)

Player and date of Albion debut	Country of birth	Albion apps	Albion goals
Glen Geard (13 November 1979)	Malta	1	0
Moshe Gariani (6 September 1980)	Israel	1	0
Jacob Cohen (18 October 1980)	Israel	6	0
Eric Young* (24 September 1983)	Singapore	148	11
Hans Kraay (27 December 1983)	Holland	23	3
Alistair Edwards (16 December 1989)	Australia	1	0
Sergei Gotsmanov (24 February 1990)	Belarus	16	4
John Robinson* (16 April 1990)	Zimbabwe	73	9
Tony Meola (1 September 1990)	United States	2	0
Igor Gurinovich (1 December 1990)	Belarus	6	2
Stefan Iovan (16 April 1991)	Romania	10	0
Juergen Sommer (16 November 1991)	United States	1	0
Junior McDougald* (13 August 1994)	United States	95	22
David Adekola (12 October 1996)	Nigeria	1	0
Valur Gislason (11 October 1997)	Iceland	7	0
Emeke Ifejiagwa (24 October 1998)	Nigeria	2	1
Lorenzo Pinamonte (18 December 1999)	Italy	9	2
Michel Kuipers (12 August 2000)	Holland	156	0

Albion's foreign players (continued)

Player and date of Albion debut	Country of birth	Albion apps	Albion goals
Dirk Lehmann (11 August 2001)	Germany	12	1
Andy Petterson (26 August 2002)	Australia	9	0
Ivar Ingimarsson (15 February 2003)	Iceland	15	0
Tony Rougier (22 February 2003)	Trinidad & Tobago	6	2
Paul Reid (12 April 2004)	Australia	83	4
Albert Jarrett* (7 August 2004)	Sierra Leone	25	1
Maheta Molango⁺ (7 August 2004)	Switzerland	6	1
David Yelldell⁺ (29 January 2005)	Germany	3	0
Rami Shabaan⁺ (19 February 2005)	Sweden	6	0
Federico Turienzo (9 August 2005)	Argentina	4	0
Seb Carole (13 August 2005)	France	42	2
Florent Chaigneau (23 August 2005)	France	3	0
Alexandre Frutos (13 September 2005)	France	37	3

All figures up to the end of 2005/06 season

* *Denotes player of British or Irish nationality.*

⁺ *Denotes player of dual nationality: Maheta Molango was born in Switzerland to an Italian mother and Congolese father; German-born David Yelldell has become an American citizen; and Rami Shabaan was born in Sweden to a Finnish mother and Egyptian father.*

NB: *Alexis Nicolas and Mark McCammon represented Cyprus (under-21s) and Barbados in international football, but both were born in London and qualified through their ancestry.*

We only need nine men

Albion fans who made the long trip north to Hull City's Boothferry Park on Tuesday 10 November 1998 left the ground singing 'We only need nine men' after they saw their team beat Hull 2-0, despite losing both Ross Johnson and Andy Arnott to red cards. Albion were two up by half-time, thanks to goals from Richie Barker and Gary Hart, but defender Johnson was sent off for a second booking ten minutes into the second half. Arnott took his place in the centre of defence, but lasted just one minute; he joined Johnson for an early bath after a professional foul in the 56th minute. The home fans sensed an easy comeback, but Albion held out for 34 minutes – and goalkeeper Mark Ormerod recorded a clean sheet.

Comic on the wing

In 1960/61 season, Albion had a certain Jimmy Tarbuck on its books. He was a Butlin's Redcoat at the nearby Ocean Hotel at Saltdean and signed on to the club staff as an amateur. Tarbuck played mainly in the club's A team on the wing or as an inside-forward, but later joked he was so one-footed he would end the season with one old boot and one boot as good as new.

Cricket at the Goldstone

Sussex played a 25-over floodlit cricket match against Surrey at the Goldstone on 7 September 1981. Sussex won by three wickets, with Imran Khan posting 123 not out for the home side.

Media moguls

A number of Albion players have forged successful careers in the media, on hanging up their boots. Mark Lawrenson – considered by many Albion fans to be the club's finest player of all time – became one of the leading pundits on the BBC, and was a regular on the channel's flagship football shows, including Football Focus and Match of the Day. Two of Lawrenson's Albion team-mates have also carved out new careers in the media following their retirement from the game. Michael Robinson was playing for Spanish side Osasuna when a knee injury forced him to quit the game. He became one of the biggest stars of Spain's sporting media as a presenter on the football show El Día Después (The Day After). Gary Stevens also made the move into reporting on the game he played with such distinction, after an injury forced him to retire. He first appeared with Sky Sports before moving on to work as a reporter and summariser on the radio station TalkSport. Hans Kraay, who played 23 times for Albion between 1983 and 1985, became a journalist in his native Holland on retirement, writing about the English game for Dutch football magazines and appearing as a presenter on Dutch TV.

Pompey reserves save Albion from relegation

In the 1903/04 season, Albion finished second-bottom of the 18-team Division One of the Southern League, after a meagre six wins from 34 matches left them a point adrift of New Brompton in the all-important third-bottom safety spot. But Albion were saved from relegation, thanks to Portsmouth's reserves. Watford had won the Second Division of the Southern League and replaced bottom-placed Kettering Town, who withdrew from the Southern League, while Pompey's second string had finished as runners-up. However, Portsmouth's first team was already in Division One (they finished fourth in 1903/04), and league rules did not allow one club to field two teams in the same division. Albion were therefore re-elected to Division One.

Baptism of fire

Albion played their first ever game in Football League Division Two away to Middlesbrough on 23 August 1958. It was a disaster, as the home team ran out 9-0 winners at Ayresome Park – a record defeat for Albion – with future Brighton manager Brian Clough scoring five of Middlesbrough's nine goals. Legend has it that Albion captain Glen Wilson knocked on the referee's dressing room door after the final whistle and asked to touch the ball, because he hadn't managed it during the entire 90 minutes of play. Despite their baptism of fire, Albion soon settled into life in Division Two and ended their debut season in a respectable 12th position in the league table – one point ahead of Middlesbrough, although the Teesiders took their tally of goals against Albion to 15 for the season with a 6-4 win at the Goldstone Ground on 20 December 1958.

Clean sheets

The club record for consecutive clean sheets is seven successive matches. Bill Hayes did it in five Division Three South matches and two FA Cup ties in 1923/24. He eventually conceded a goal when Queen's Park Rangers's Richard Parker scored in a 1-0 win for Rangers on 19 January 1924. A season later, Hayes equalled his own run of five Football League matches without conceding, a personal record also matched by Brian Powney (1970), Peter Grummitt (1977), Nicky Rust (1995) and Ben Roberts (2004). The club record for league matches is six. In 2000, Michel Kuipers and Mark Cartwright both kept goal in the six-match run.

Four plus three equals seven

The most amazing 28 minutes of football in the club's history were without doubt the minutes in which Albion hit seven second-half goals – all scored by Peter Ward and Ian Mellor – in a Division Three match with Walsall on Tuesday 5 October 1976. The first half gave no indication of what was to come after the half-time interval. The first 45 minutes, at a miserable, snow- and rain-swept Goldstone Ground, had been a disappointing and drab affair. Unsurprisingly, the team were lambasted by Alan Mullery, who sent teacups crashing around the dressing room in one of his trademark half-time tirades and sent the players out early for the second half. They stood in the centre circle in the pouring rain with their manager's words still ringing in their ears, waiting for Walsall to appear. The roasting did the trick. A devastating 28-minute spell saw Ward hit four goals and Mellor a hat trick, and the 14,128-strong crowd that braved the elements on a pig of a night got the ultimate reward. Mullery later explained in an interview with *The Argus*, 'It started with a phone call from Glen Wilson, who was our kit man at the time, saying it was snowing and the club didn't have any orange footballs. I couldn't believe it and went to a local sports shop in Surrey where I lived at the time and brought some down. I wasn't smiling later on. There were some 15,000 fans inside the Goldstone – of which two-thirds were uncovered – and the fans were standing there getting soaked in diabolical conditions. They watched a terrible first half, which was like a practice match. We got to their 18-yard line and gave the ball away and they did likewise at the other end. At half-time the team were about to have some tea, but I threw all the tea cups up the wall and sent the players out into the centre circle to stand in the snow and rain and feel what the fans were feeling. Within 25 minutes they'd scored seven goals, with Peter Ward getting four and Ian Mellor three.'

French connection

The old adage that you wait hours for a bus then two or three turn up at once could easily be applied to Albion when it comes to French players. In the first 105 years of the club's history, not one man from a country that's nearer to Brighton and Hove than Birmingham, Manchester or Liverpool (all towns from which Albion sourced several players in those 105 years) had made the trip across the English Channel. That was until 12 August 2005, when winger Sebastien Carole signed from Monaco and goalkeeper Florent Chaigneau joined on loan from Rennes. By 31 August, when Alex Frutos arrived from Metz, the French contingent numbered three.

Limited company

Brighton & Hove Albion Football Club became a limited company at a meeting in Brighton's Royal Pavilion on 11 April 1904, when the club's committee and supporters voted unanimously in favour of the move and a subsequent share floatation. George Broadbridge was the first chairman of The Brighton & Hove Albion Football Club Limited, the name under which the limited liability company was registered with Companies House on 27 May 1904. The company offices were listed as 129 Church Road, Hove. In addition to Broadbridge, the board of directors was made up of Reg Alderton, Charles Bunker, Tom Cooter, Frederick Stevens, Albert Grinyer (licensee at the Albion Inn) and Ben Parker. The club's Articles of Association forbid the men from receiving remuneration, and included a non-profit clause forbidding any board member to retain any financial residue left over, should the club fold (a clause removed by the board following the takeover by Bill Archer and Greg Stanley in the 1990s). Soon afterwards, Bunker and Grinyer stepped down and William Baker, Noah Clark, Richard Merriman and Harry Gadd, the owner of the Albion Hotel and Albion Coffee House, joined the board. With shares also available to the general public, Albion's new board held 1460 of the 4078 shares allotted in the floatation; Ben Parker was the major shareholder with 480 shares, which cost him an investment of £120.

We Are Brighton

Since the late 1970s, We Are Brighton has been a popular terrace chant with Albion supporters. The song was born when Rod Stewart's hit record Sailing was adapted. The tune remains one of the most popular with Albion supporters and is still sung today. In 2002, a book called *We Are Brighton* was published, charting the club's back-to-back championships of 2000/01 and 2001/02. The song is sung as follows:

> *We are Brighton*
> *We are Brighton*
> *Super Brighton from the south*
> *We are Brighton*
> *Super Brighton*
> *We are Brighton from the south*

Records for goals in a season

Albion's record holder for most goals scored in one season is Peter Ward. He managed a haul of 36 in all competitions during the 1976/77 season, as he helped Albion win promotion from Division Three. Ward also scored a record number of league goals (32) in the same season. Frank McAvoy (see 'First ever hard man', page 63) was Albion's original leading goal-scorer, hitting nine goals (six in the 11 Southern League games he played for the club) during the club's first ever season of 1901/02. The following year, Frank Scott managed 31 in all competitions (11 of which came in the Southern League). Frank Hall was the first to score 20-plus league goals, and three players achieved 25 league goals in a season: Jimmy Smith, Tommy Cook (twice, in the 1920s, by which time the Albion was a member of the Football League) and Sam Jennings. In 1929/30, former Aston Villa and Queen's Park Rangers centre forward Hugh Vallance became the first to hit 30 league goals in his only full season with the club. His record tally of league goals stood for 47 years until Ward topped it. Although Arthur Attwood (who scored a breathtaking 75 goals in 104 Albion appearances) beat Ward's all-competitions total in 1932/33, there were slightly extenuating circumstances as four of his goals came in the FA Cup qualifying rounds (see 'FA Cup records', page 53). Other Albion players to have enjoyed 30-plus seasons are Dan Kirkwood, who hit 31 goals in all competitions in the same season that Vallance set his scoring record;

Garry Nelson, who hit 32 in the promotion season of 1987/88; and Bobby Zamora, who matched Kirkwood's and Nelson's totals in successive seasons, becoming the first player ever to score 30-plus goals in two separate seasons. Zamora hit 31 goals in all competitions as Albion won the Third Division title in 2000/01, then bagged 32 in all competitions as Albion won a second successive title, the Second Division championship, the following season.

Most goals in a season

Record holders	League goals	Total goals	Season
Frank McAvoy	6	9	1901/02
Frank Scott	11	31	1902/03
Jack Hall	22	28	1906/07
Jimmy Smith	25	27	1911/12
Tommy Cook	25	28	1923/24
Sam Jennings	25	27	1926/27
Tommy Cook	25	26	1927/28
Hugh Vallance	30	32	1929/30
Arthur Attwood	20	35	1932/33
Peter Ward	32	36	1976/77

Maheta's 12-second impact

Swiss-born striker Maheta Molango scored the quickest goal on record in the club's history when he took just 12 seconds to put Albion ahead at Reading on the opening day of the 2004/05 season. Molango, who speaks five languages and studied to become a lawyer in the early days of his football career, was making his debut for the club, after earning a contract with an impressive haul of five goals in the 2004 pre-season campaign. While Maheta's goal is the quickest with an official recorded time, a goal scored in wartime football by Cyril Hodges against Millwall at the Goldstone on 17 February 1945 is believed to have been two seconds faster. Hodges was an Arsenal player at the time and was guesting for Albion in the match, although he later joined Albion as a player and even became a coach at the club. After kicking off, Hodges ran on to collect a pass from Frank O'Donnell and fired home the first of four goals in the 6-2 win. The press gave the time as ten seconds.

Scandal number one

John Jackson was one of the main driving forces behind the birth of
the Albion – he's often referred to as the founder of the club – and
he became the first ever manager when the club was formed in 1901.
He led the club to their first promotion in 1902/03, to the Southern
League Division One as joint winners of Division Two, but left the
club under a cloud in March 1905. At an extraordinary general
meeting, and amid accusations of financial irregularities, it emerged
that the club accounts were in disarray. Nothing had been logged
since January 1905 and, despite an eloquent denial from Jackson at
the EGM, both he and secretary Charles Campbell paid with their
jobs. In April, the Football Association began an investigation into
the club's finances and suspended George Broadbridge, Noah Clark,
Harry Gadd, Ben Parker and Frederick Stevens for illegal payments
to an amateur player (clubs were strictly forbidden from paying
amateurs any more than their expenses). The player in question, the
goalkeeper GL Robinson, also received a three-month ban. As a
result, Albion brought in Frank Walford-Scott (see 'Scandal number
two', page 86) and restructured the board the following season.

Fanzines

Fans were offered an alternative to the match programme in 1988,
as the first fanzines dedicated to events at the Albion were published
at the start of the 1988/89 season. *And Smith Must Score* was an A4
publication that ran until 1992, but it was the A5 tabloid-style *Gulls
Eye* that grabbed the headlines, often for the wrong reasons. A too-
close-to-the-bone front cover in the wake of the Kegworth air
disaster was in bad taste and made headlines in the national tabloid
newspapers. In 1990, *Gulls Eye* was back in the national news when
it was sued by three of the club's directors after an article questioned
their integrity. The matter was eventually settled out of court for a
sum of £6000. Despite the bad press, *Gulls Eye* always fought the
fans' corner and its most notable success was the launch of
Brighton's Independent Supporters' Association (BISA) which was
behind the fight to save the Goldstone Ground and the eventually
successful bid to remove the unpopular chairman Bill Archer and
chief executive David Bellotti in the late 1990s. The last ever issue of
Gulls Eye coincided with Albion's last ever game at the Goldstone.
Other fanzines included *Pretty In Pink, A Rat In The Camp, On The*

Up, Scars & Stripes, Build A Bonfire, Come Over The Dyke, One F in Falmer, Keep the Faith, Brighton Rockz, Nine-Nil, Seaside Saga, The Tommy Cook Report and a relaunched *Gulls Eye II* (under new editors), but it was the original *Gulls Eye*, which reached 100 issues, that was the most prolific of Albion fanzines.

Champions I

Albion won their first ever championship when they became Southern League champions in 1909/10. They finished five points clear of second-placed Swindon Town, against whom they clinched the title with a 3-1 win in the penultimate game of the season on 23 April 1910. Bill 'Bullet' Jones hit two goals that afternoon, with Bert Longstaff getting the third. Albion's first ever first-place finish was a vast improvement on the previous season of 1908/09, when Albion had finished one place above the relegation zone and stayed up on goal average. The top of the 22-team 1909/10 table looked like this:

Southern League Division One 1909/10

Team	P	W	D	L	F	A	W	D	L	F	A	Points
Albion	42	18	2	1	50	11	5	11	5	19	17	59
Swindon Town	42	15	3	3	63	20	7	7	7	29	26	54
QPR	42	12	5	4	41	28	7	8	6	15	19	51
Northampton	42	16	3	2	66	11	6	1	14	24	33	48

Born on a match day

Six of Albion's current first-team squad (at the start of the 2006/07 season) were born on a day when the club's first team was in action. Captain Charlie Oatway's date of birth should be considered a great day in the club's history, but older fans may be forgiven for having erased 28 November 1973 from their minds. When Charlie was coming into the world at Hammersmith Hospital, Albion were suffering possibly the most embarrassing result in the club's history some 64 miles down the road, in the shape of a 4-0 drubbing by non-league minnows Walton & Hersham in an FA Cup first-round replay at the Goldstone Ground. Richard Carpenter, Chris Breach, Joel Lynch and Tommy Fraser were also born on Albion match days, but perhaps the most quirky tale is that of Joe Gatting, who was born on the day Albion tackled Southend United in an Associate Members' Cup (now the Football League Trophy) match at the Goldstone Ground. Wearing the number 6 shirt that evening was Joe's father, Steve.

Players born on match days

Guy Butters *30 October 1969*
1 November: Division Three v Fulham 2-1 (h)

Richard Carpenter *30 September 1972*
30 September: Division Two v Portsmouth 0-2 (a)

Charlie Oatway *28 November 1973*
28 November: FA Cup (1RR) v Walton & Hersham 0-4 (h)

Michel Kuipers *26 June 1974*
17 August: Division Three v Crystal Palace 1-0 (h)

Gary Hart *21 September 1976*
22 September: League Cup (3R) v West Bromwich Albion 2-1 (a)

Kerry Mayo *21 September 1977*
24 September: Division Two v Sheffield United 2-1 (h)

Paul Reid *6 July 1979*
18 August: Division One v Arsenal 0-4 (h)

Alex Frutos *23 April 1982*
24 April: Division One v Manchester United 0-1 (h)

Maheta Molango *24 July 1982*
28 August: Division One v Ipswich Town 1-1 (h)

Dean Hammond *7 March 1983*
12 March: FA Cup (QF) v Norwich City 1-0 (h)

Alex Revell *7 July 1983*
27 August: Division Two v Oldham Athletic 0-1 (a)

Wayne Henderson *16 September 1983*
17 September: Division Two v Carlisle United 1-1 (h)

Adam Hinshelwood *8 January 1984*
14 January: Division Two v Oldham Athletic 4-0 (h)

Adam El-Abd *11 September 1984*
15 September: Division Two v Crystal Palace 1-0 (h)

Albert Jarrett *23 October 1984*
27 October: Division Two v Shrewsbury Town 0-0 (a)

Chris Breach *19 April 1986*
19 April: Division Two v Sunderland 1-1 (a)

Jake Robinson *23 October 1986*
25 October: Division Two v Derby County 1-4 (a)

Doug Loft	25 December 1986
	26 December: Division Two v Crystal Palace 0-2 (a)
Sam Rents	22 June 1987
	15 August: Division Three v York City 1-0 (h)
Dean Cox	12 August 1987
	15 August: Division Three v York City 1-0 (h)
Richard Martin	1 September 1987
	5 September: Division Three v Blackpool 1-3 (h)
Tommy Elphick	7 September 1987
	12 September: Division Three v Aldershot 4-1 (a)
Joel Lynch	3 October 1987
	3 October: Division Three v Bury 2-1 (h)
Paul Hinshelwood	11 October 1987
	17 October: Division Three v Preston North End 0-0 (h)
Joe Gatting	25 November 1987
	25 November: AMC group game v Southend United 3-2 (h)
Tommy Fraser	5 December 1987
	5 December: FA Cup (2R) v Northampton Town 2-1 (a)
Scott Chamberlain	15 January 1988
	16 January: Division Three v Sunderland 0-1 (a)
John Sullivan	8 March 1988
	9 March: AMC (QF) v Notts County 1-5 (h)
Wes Fogden	12 April 1988
	15 April: Division Three v Northampton Town 3-0 (h)

Champions of all England

In 1910, Albion won the Southern League Division One championship (see 'Champions I', page 21), and in doing so they earned the right to tackle Football League championship winners Aston Villa in the Charity Shield at Stamford Bridge at the start of the 1910/11 season. The winners of the match between the Southern League champions and Football League champions were usually referred to as the 'Champions of England'. Albion were the underdogs; the Football League was considered a much more competitive competition. However, Albion produced a major shock by winning 1-0. Charlie Webb scored the winner, collecting a pass from Bill Hastings and firing into the net. The win was the biggest achievement in the club's history at the time, and it has probably only been surpassed by Albion's promotion to the top division of English football in 1979 and the club's appearance in the 1983 FA Cup Final. The team line-up on the day was: Bob Whiting; Fred Blackman, Joe Leeming; Billy Booth, Joe McGhie, Jack Haworth; Bert Longstaff, Jimmy Coleman, Bullet Jones, Charlie Webb, Bill Hastings.

Good Old Sussex by the Sea

Sussex by the Sea, a military marching song composed by W Ward-Higgs for the Sussex Regiment in World War 1, has been considered the club's anthem for many years. The team run out to the music at every home match, supporters can download it from the club's website as a ring-tone for mobile phones and in recent years supporters have recorded their own versions or remixes. The earliest record of supporters singing the tune in homage to the Albion comes from a report in the *Sussex Daily News* in 1911. Following an FA Cup victory at Leeds City on Saturday 14 January, around 2000 supporters gathered in the concourse of Brighton Station and at 1.45 in the early hours of 15 January 1911, sang Good Old Brighton by the Sea to welcome their victorious heroes home. In February 1965, comedian Norman Wisdom (then a director of the club) was commissioned to rewrite the lyrics to give them an Albion theme. They were printed in the programme for the match against Chesterfield on Saturday 27 February at the Goldstone, and sung at half-time:

> *We're the team from Sussex*
> *Sussex by the sea*
> *Eleven players and a crowd who roar them to victory*
> *So shout you fans and make 'em score (Goal!)*
> *Clap your hands until they're sore [clap clap clap]*
> *'Cause we're going up and we'll win the Cup*
> *For Albion by the shore*

> *We're the team from Brighton*
> *Hove, by Jove, that's us*
> *We're always fair, we never swear, but now it's hit or bust!!*
> *So shout you fans and make 'em score (Goal!)*
> *Clap your hands until they're sore [clap clap clap]*
> *'Cause we're going up and we'll win the Cup*
> *For Albion by the shore*

Wisdom's lyrics live on in the shortened version which fans can often be heard singing at matches:

> *Good old Sussex by the sea*
> *For we're going up and we'll win the Cup*
> *For Sussex by the sea*
> *Altogether now…*
> *Good old Sussex by the sea*
> *Good old Sussex by the sea*
> *For we're going up and we'll win the Cup*
> *For Sussex by the sea*

Sussex Cricket Club's fans also use Sussex By The Sea as their anthem, and in 1957 Joe Haddon rewrote special lyrics for the cricket club. However, Sussex fans now sing the shortened version and it is now a tradition for the Sussex squad to sing this very loudly in the dressing room following each victory. The player who has contributed most to the game, nominated by coach or captain, has the honour of leading the singing.

Fiercest rivals

Albion's nearest club and fiercest rivals are Crystal Palace, 44 miles up the A23 and M23 in Croydon. (The next nearest league club is Portsmouth, 47 miles away.) Considering the distance between the clubs, some fans cannot understand how the rivalry with Crystal Palace developed. For the history, you have to go back to the opening day of the 1974/75 season, 17 August. Palace were the visitors to the Goldstone Ground and Albion won 1-0, but minor skirmishes before the game ended in some 20 arrests. The rivalry continued to develop over the next few seasons, but it really took off in 1976/77. The clubs were the two biggest in Division Three at the time and, in a season that saw them competing for the Third Division championship, they also met three times in the FA Cup. A 1-1 draw at the Goldstone Ground in October was a tame affair in comparison to what was to come when the two clubs were drawn together in the first round of the FA Cup. On 20 November 1976, Palace drew 2-2 at the Goldstone. The replay at Selhurst Park three days later also finished all square at 1-1, meaning a second replay would take place at Stamford Bridge on Monday 6 December. It was a highly controversial affair, with Phil Holder scoring the winner for Palace. Albion boss Alan Mullery wasn't a happy man, after captain Brian Horton scored from the penalty spot only to see referee Ron Challis rule the effort out for encroachment. After being pelted with beer cans by the Crystal Palace supporters, Mullery flicked a V-sign at them, for which the Football Association later fined him £75. Albion and Palace were both promoted, in second and third place respectively. Two seasons later, the clubs were promoted together again, to Division One, with Palace as champions and Albion runners-up.

Top flight record

Having played 156 Division One matches for the club, Steve Foster holds the club record for the highest number of appearances in an Albion shirt in the top flight of English football. Such was Foster's consistency that he missed just 12 games during Albion's four seasons in the First Division.

Songs for our rivals

There are the stock offerings of 'We hate Palace' and 'If you all hate Palace clap your hands'. With a match against Palace often taking place on Boxing Day, it's no surprise that some of the more creative anti-Palace chants have a festive flavour:

Away in a manger
No crib for a bed
The little lord Jesus
Sat up and he said
We hate Palace and we hate Palace!
We hate Palace and we hate Palace!
We are the Palace haters!

Hark now hear
The Brighton sing
The Palace run away… again!
And we will fight for ever more
Because of Boxing Day

According to club historian Tim Carder, this was first heard at the Goldstone Ground on Boxing Day 1979 when Albion beat Crystal

Palace 3-0, with goals from Brian Horton, Peter Ward and Gerry Ryan. The fans had good reason to celebrate, as it was Albion's first win over Palace in 10 games. The song has been sung ever since. Palace try to claim it as their own, but as they didn't beat Albion on Boxing Day until 1986 (by which time Albion had given Palace three Boxing Day tankings) it's a rather hollow claim. Another anti-Palace chant is the imaginative reworking of the Terry Jacks song, Seasons in the Sun:

> We had joy
> We had fun
> We had Palace on the run
> But the fun didn't last
> 'Cause the b******s ran too fast

A quick profit

Adam Virgo's transfer from Albion to Celtic in July 2005 represented Albion's biggest profit on a single player. The Brighton-born defender cost the club nothing in terms of a transfer fee when he signed professional forms after joining the club straight from Ardingly College in the summer of 2000. His move to Parkhead five years later equalled the club's record transfer fee ever received, and earned Albion a clear profit of £1.5m. However, the quickest profit on any player was the £110,000 the club netted when midfielder Paul Holsgrove moved from Albion to Hibernian in August 1998, just 39 days after signing for the Seagulls on a free transfer from Stoke City, and after having played just one friendly match (at Lewes) in Albion colours. On 23 June 1998, Albion's then-boss Brian Horton, quite probably well aware of the interest from north of the border, met Holsgrove at the club's training ground and shrewdly convinced the former Reading player to sign for Albion before returning home. Hibs boss Alex McLeish, who was on summer vacation when Holsgrove joined Albion, had also expressed a keen interest in the player and had left clear instructions for the club to sign Holsgrove in his absence. He returned home to learn that Albion had beaten the Scottish Premier Leaguers to it and was left with no choice but to prise his man away by offering a fee. Eventually, Albion reluctantly accepted £110,000 for a man who had never played a senior first-team game for the club.

First ever league match

Albion's first ever Football League match took place against Southend United at their Kursaal Ground on 28 August 1920. The match ended in a 2-0 win for the home team, but in the days when home and away fixtures against an opposing club were more often than not played back to back, Albion gained revenge a week later by beating Southend 1-0 at the Goldstone Ground, courtesy of a Jack Doran goal. In those days, teams played the WM formation and the Albion line-up for the first ever league match was:

Ted Rogerson (OL) Jack Doran (CF) George Ritchie (OR)

Zacky March (IL) Bert Longstaff (IR)

Harry Bentley (HB) Fretwell Hall (HB)

George Coomber (HB)

Wally Little (FB) Jack Woodhouse (FB)

Billy Hayes (GK)

Key:

GK – *goalkeeper;* **FB** – *full-back;* **HB** – *half-back;* **IR** – *inside-right;* **IL** – *inside-left;* **OR** – *outside-right;* **CF** – *centre forward;* **OL** – *outside-left*

People's Player I

On 7 December 1970, with very little cash in his transfer kitty, Albion manager Pat Saward launched the Buy a Player fund. The initial aim was to raise £50,000 to help strengthen a team embroiled in a relegation scrap at the bottom of the Third Division. The public's reaction to the launch was indifferent and the club's finances came under scrutiny from some, but the majority of supporters got behind Saward's idea. The scheme did not meet its target, although it did raise enough to pay £10,000 to Birmingham City for the services of Bert Murray. Midfielder Murray was already on loan at the Goldstone Ground from City, and Saward sealed Murray's permanent switch using cash from the fund, despite interest from promotion-chasing Third Division rivals Fulham. Murray was immediately christened 'The People's Player' by supporters, and he lived up to his billing. His arrival proved to be the turning point in Albion's season. Lying 23rd (one place from the bottom) when Murray arrived, Albion lost just five of their 18 remaining matches. Midfielder Murray even weighed in with four goals. The following season, Murray's 13 goals from midfield, in a season in which he missed just one match, helped Albion win promotion as runners-up to Aston Villa in May 1972. Murray eventually left Albion when he joined Peterborough United for £6000 in September 1973, having made 109 appearances and scored 26 goals.

England caretaker bosses

Two of England's caretaker bosses in recent years have had Albion connections. Howard Wilkinson (who played 147 matches for Albion, scoring 19 goals) took charge of the national team on two separate occasions, first following the sacking of Glenn Hoddle in 1999, then after Kevin Keegan's resignation a year later. Wilkinson was in charge for the 2-0 friendly defeat against France at Wembley on 10 February 1999 and for the World Cup qualifier against Finland in Helsinki on 11 October 2000. For the next match against Italy on 15 November 2000, the Football Association turned to Leicester City manager Peter Taylor, who took charge for the friendly match in Turin. (Less than a year later, he became Albion boss.) England lost the game 1-0, but Taylor made the historic decision to hand David Beckham the England captaincy for the first time.

First Football League season

Albion first became a member of the Football League when they competed in the inaugural season of the newly formed Division Three South in 1920/21. Albion ended the season in 18th position, with 36 points largely picked up at the Goldstone Ground, where Albion lost just four times in the league. Irish international Jack Doran was top scorer with 21 league goals. The club has retained its league status ever since (for the complete record, see 'Albion's Football League record', page 82) although it was forced to seek re-election in 1948 when Albion suffered their worst ever season and finished bottom of the Fourth Division.

Football League Third Division South 1920/21

Team	P	W	D	L	F	A	W	D	L	F	A	Points
Crystal Palace	42	15	4	2	45	17	9	7	5	25	17	59
Southampton	42	14	5	2	46	10	5	11	5	18	18	54
QPR	42	14	4	3	38	11	8	5	8	23	21	53
Swindon Town	42	14	5	2	51	17	7	5	9	22	32	52
Swansea Town	42	9	10	2	32	19	9	5	7	24	26	51
Watford	42	14	4	3	40	15	6	4	11	19	29	48
Millwall	42	11	5	5	25	8	7	6	8	17	22	47
Merthyr Town	42	13	5	3	46	20	2	10	9	14	29	45
Luton Town	42	14	6	1	51	15	2	6	13	10	41	44
Bristol Rovers	42	15	3	3	51	22	3	4	14	17	35	43
Plymouth Argyle	42	10	7	4	25	13	1	14	6	10	21	43

	P	W	D	L	F	A	W	D	L	F	A	Pts
Portsmouth	42	10	8	3	28	14	2	7	12	18	34	39
Grimsby Town	42	12	5	4	32	16	3	4	14	17	43	39
Northampton Town	42	11	4	6	32	23	4	4	13	27	52	38
Newport County	42	8	5	8	20	23	6	4	11	23	41	37
Norwich City	42	9	10	2	31	14	1	6	14	13	39	36
Southend United	42	13	2	6	32	20	1	6	14	12	41	36
Albion	42	11	6	4	28	20	3	2	16	14	41	36
Exeter City	42	9	7	5	27	15	1	8	12	12	39	35
Reading	42	8	4	9	26	22	4	3	14	16	37	31
Brentford	42	7	9	5	27	23	2	3	16	15	44	30
Gillingham	42	6	9	6	19	24	2	3	16	15	50	28

First five-figure average

Albion enjoyed their first five-figure average crowd in the 1936/37 season as Albion finished third in Division Three South. During the season, 224,008 fans flocked to the Goldstone Ground, an average of 10,667 across the 21 games. The average was down the following season (but not by much), to 10,164. The average crowd dropped below 10,000 to 8392 in 1938/39, then dropped drastically during the Second World War to less than 5000. It didn't hit five figures again until the 1947/48 season.

Lowest ever crowd

With the exception of wartime and some of Albion's early Southern League matches, the club's lowest ever home crowd was the paltry attendance of 1073. The small crowd turned out for a League Cup tie against Leyton Orient on 13 August 1997, during the disastrous ground-share at Gillingham's Priestfield Stadium. The lowest ever crowd for a Football League match, also at Gillingham, was just 1025 for a match with Barnet on 5 December 1997. The lowest crowd for a Football League fixture at the Goldstone Ground came from the same era, as fans protested against the sale of the Goldstone Ground by boycotting a match with Mansfield Town on 9 November 1996. The official attendance was 1933. Thousands of fans descended on Hove, but protested by remaining outside in Hove Park. At half-time, several hundred of them broke into the unused East Terrace through an exit gate and peacefully invaded the pitch. Albion were trailing 1-0 at the interval, but after the fans had cleared the pitch, a rousing second half saw Denny Mundee equalise for the Seagulls to win what would turn out to be a vital point.

Match of the Day 1972

The Match of the Day cameras were at the Goldstone Ground for Albion's meeting with Third Division leaders Aston Villa on 25 March 1972. Pat Saward's side were third in the table, but their promotion push was in danger of fizzling out after back-to-back defeats to mid-table Oldham Athletic and lowly Bradford City immediately prior to high-flying Villa's visit. Albion took the lead with a brilliant team goal scored by Willie Irvine (which came third in the BBC's Goal of the Season competition), and a second-half goal from Kit Napier helped Albion to a 2-1 win over the eventual champions. The win was vital for Albion, who finished runners-up to Aston Villa in the other promotion place, three points clear of third-placed Bournemouth.

Make some noise

With four matches left to play at the end of the 2004/05 season, Albion were in the championship relegation zone, but still had plenty to play for. The local paper *The Argus* launched the Make Some Noise campaign, which urged supporters to do exactly that. The campaign seemed to do the trick, as Albion remained unbeaten for the rest of the season, picking up draws at Burnley and at home to Leicester City and West Ham United. The three draws were followed by a vital away win at Rotherham United, before a final-day draw at home to Ipswich Town secured Albion's survival.

Corinthian Casuals clash captures the imagination

Albion were drawn against the legendary touring side the Corinthian Casuals in the first round of the 1922/23 FA Cup, and the three matches attracted nationwide interest. The famous amateur club had been formed in 1882 with the aim of helping to improve England's national team, and was largely made up of public school boys and university players. They originally had a strict amateur code, with their club rules stating that the team would only play friendly matches. However, those rules were amended by club officials in time for the 1922/23 season, to allow the club entry into the FA Cup. Because of their status across the country, the Football Association exempted them from the qualifying rounds and, for their first FA Cup tie in round one of the competition, they were paired with Albion. On 13 January 1923, Corinthian Casuals, packed with amateur and full internationals, arrived at the Goldstone Ground. Albion boss Charlie Webb considered his side to be underdogs, so he must have been delighted when Andy Neil equalised Norman Creek's opener for the amateurs. The first replay (at Crystal Palace, the home of the Cup Final in the early 1900s) also ended in a 1-1 draw after extra time, this time with Tommy Cook the scorer. Albion were allowed to choose the venue for the second replay, and selected Stamford Bridge. A crowd of 43,760 packed in to watch the match (a huge number for a midweek afternoon match at a neutral ground) and saw Tommy Cook score a second-half winner to put them into the second round. Such was the national interest that cine-film of the first match at the Goldstone was shown in cinemas across the country and a special souvenir card of the game was produced for sale.

Record transfer fee received I

The £700 that Middlesbrough paid Albion for centre forward Jack Hall in April 1908 became a club record fee received, but the move landed Middlesbrough in hot water with the Football Association. Hall arrived from Football League outfit Stoke City in May 1906 and scored 54 goals in 93 games for Albion in all competitions (Southern League, United League, Western League, Southern Section Cup and FA Cup). Middlesbrough offered Albion £700, even though the maximum transfer fee in 1908 was £350. They got round this by offering the money for both Hall and a 'makeweight' (in the deal, half-back Harry Kent). Middlesbrough were fined an additional £100 by the FA when Stoke City protested that they still held the player's Football League registration.

Spurs 0 Southampton 0

Going into the final day of the 1977/78 season on 29 April, Albion were still in a position to win promotion to Division One, but it would require an Albion win at home to Blackpool, coupled with a win for either of the teams in the Southampton v Tottenham Hotspur game taking place at the same time. A capacity crowd of 33,431 saw Albion keep their end of the bargain, but the hope that either Spurs or Southampton would produce a victory was misguided. The two teams, unsurprisingly, played out a goalless draw that ensured promotion for both clubs.

Most league doubles in a season

The club record for the highest number of doubles (beating the same club both home and away) in a season is eight. Albion achieved this in three separate seasons: in 1936/37, when the team finished third in Division Three South, and the championship-winning seasons of 1957/58 and 1964/65. The other championship seasons of 2000/01 and 2001/02 saw Albion record seven and five doubles respectively.

The Blaydon Races

Newcastle United fans sing the Blaydon Races, which dates from the early 1970s. In the same era, Albion fans adapted the Magpies' version to suit their own team (nowadays, fans sing 'Brighton aces' in the final line):

> *Oh the lads*
> *You should have seen us coming*
> *Everywhere was blue and white and everyone was running*
> *All the lads and lasses, all with smiling faces*
> *Going down the Shoreham Road*
> *To see Pat Saward's aces*

Albion's first black player

Albion's first black player was Londoner Dave Busby. He went to school at Heathfield in Sussex and it was while playing for Heathfield United that he came to the attention of Albion – spotted by backroom staff Joe and Glen Wilson. He joined Albion as an apprentice in 1973 and made his debut on 20 October that year, coming on as a substitute in Pat Saward's last match as Albion manager, a 2-0 win over Shrewsbury Town. After Brian Clough took charge of Albion Busby didn't play again that season, but impressed enough in the reserves to be offered a professional contract. He made just three further first-team appearances in 1974/75, however, (two as a substitute) and was released in May 1975 to join Worthing.

Do or die day at Hereford

Albion's match with Hereford United on 3 May 1997 was the antithesis of the famous Liverpool v Arsenal clash at the end of the 1988/89 season, which saw the Gunners snatch the title from their Mersey rivals on the final day of the season at Anfield. As the Albion team travelled to Edgar Street for their final match of the 1996/97 season, they did so in the knowledge that a defeat would cost them their league status and quite possibly the club's very existence. A win or a draw would be enough to keep Albion (who in December had been 12 points adrift at the foot of the table) in the Football League, but would relegate their hosts. The scenario was hardly conducive to a game of flowing football, with both teams desperate not to make the mistake that might prove terminal. Disaster struck for Albion after 20 minutes when Kerry Mayo made the ultimate error and put the ball through his own goal. The mood amongst Albion supporters was sombre during the half-time interval, but a wave of optimism swept through the visiting fans just prior to the start of the second half. After 55 minutes, Albion were forced to replace winger Paul McDonald, who had picked up an injury. The switch transformed the game as, seven minutes later, substitute Robbie Reinelt scored an equaliser. Albion clung on for the remaining 28 minutes, despite a scare as Adrian Foster raced clean through in the final moments of the game but was denied by a save by Albion keeper Mark Ormerod. The draw preserved Albion's league status, and sent Hereford down to the Conference. The Albion line up on the day was:

Subs: *Robbie Reinelt (for McDonald), Dave Martin, Gary Hobson.*

Goldstone bought

Until 1926, Albion had sublet the Goldstone Ground from Alderman John Clark, who in turn leased the ground from the Stanford Estate. Under this arrangement, all fixtures and fittings – the South and West Stands, dressing rooms and other structures – were the property of Clark, meaning that any developments Albion did had to be carried out via Clark and then rented to the club as part of the overall package. This complicated arrangement ended on 26 September 1926, when Albion chairman Charles Brown agreed that the club would pay Clark compensation for the remaining five years of his lease and buy the permanent structures on the ground. In a very shrewd move, he also agreed a new 99-year lease direct with the Stanford Estate, with an option for the club to buy the site themselves within the next eight years. Albion completed the purchase for the sum of £5120 in the summer of 1930. Over the next few months, work was carried out to improve the dilapidated wooden West Stand to meet with local authority requirements, and a roof was put up over three-quarters of the terracing behind the north goal. The work was completed in January 1931, the new North Stand roof having been paid for with money raised by the supporters' club.

World Cup rejects

Three players who went to the 2006 World Cup Finals in Germany had previously not been considered good enough for Albion. Swedish goalkeeper Rami Shaaban and Trinidad & Tobago pair Kelvin Jack and Brent Sancho had all played matches for Albion in 2005. Former Arsenal and West Ham goalkeeper Shabaan signed on a short-term contract in February 2005 and played six games towards the end of the 2004/05 season. The early signs had been good, as Shabaan helped Albion record victories over eventual champions Sunderland and Millwall. His form nose-dived, however, and he conceded 12 goals in his next four matches. He was dropped from the side and in the summer of 2005 was not offered a new contract by the club. He returned to his homeland and signed for Fredrikstad, where his form earned him a call up to the Swedish World Cup squad, and when first-choice keeper Andreas Isaksson was injured in training, Shabaan got selected for the first match. He kept a clean sheet in the goalless draw with Trinidad & Tobago, and lining up in opposition for the Soca Warriors was Sancho, who had played two friendly matches against

Lewes and Colchester United while on trial with Albion in July 2005. The central defender (who eventually signed for Gillingham in 2005) also played in the games against England (0-2) and Paraguay (1-2). Goalkeeper Jack (who played trial matches for Albion against Colchester United and Bognor Regis Town) should have played in the opening game too, but injured himself in the pre-match warm up and had to wait for Trinidad & Tobago's final game against Paraguay for his World Cup debut.

Shortest and longest names

While Charlie Oatway easily has the longest full name of any in the club's history (see 'Biggest name in football', page 57) the player with the longest surname was on-loan forward Michael Mahoney-Johnson (thankfully in the days before names were written on the back of shirts), who made four appearances without scoring a goal during a month's loan spell in February 1998. The longest single-barrelled surname was 12 letters long and there have been three such players for Albion: Les Champelovier, Peter Downsborough and George Featherstone. As for the shortest, there have been a number of players with three-letter surnames: Dean Cox, Albert Day, Mark Fox, Reg Fox, Simon Fox, Joe Jee, Alec Law, Barney Lee, David Lee, George Ley, Chris May, Larry May, Gordon Mee, Jock Sim and Harold Sly, to list them all.

Princes versus paupers

When Albion met Tottenham Hotspur in the FA Cup third round at White Hart Line on 8 January 2005, there was a gulf of over £23m between the club's respective starting line-ups. The total cost of Albion's starting XI was £61,000 (plus a set of kit) and their most expensive player was Leon Knight. Although free on arrival from Chelsea in 2003, he had cost Albion a payment of £50,000 when they won promotion in 2004. Spurs, on the other hand, had paid transfer fees of at least £23.45m for their line-up, and that figure didn't include the fee paid for Reto Ziegler, believed to be in the region of £1m. Robbie Keane and Jermain Defoe – a former team-mate of Knight's at the famous London junior boys football club Senrab – were the most expensive players on the pitch. Spurs had paid £7m for each of them, although Keane had switched clubs (including Leeds United and Inter Milan) for fees totalling £38m.

Despite the difference on the balance sheet, Albion more than matched their hosts on the pitch. Ledley King opened the scoring in the first half, before Richard Carpenter fired a free kick past England keeper Paul Robinson early in the second half. With Albion just seven minutes from taking Spurs to a replay, Keane showed exactly why all those millions of pounds had been spent on acquiring his services, by scoring a wonderful winning goal.

Spurs v Albion 2005: The respective teams and costs

Albion	Fee paid	Spurs	Fee paid
Michel Kuipers	Free transfer	Paul Robinson	£1.5m
Paul Reid	Free transfer	Erik Edman	£1.7m
Adam Hinshelwood	Trainee	Ledley King	Trainee
Guy Butters	Free transfer	Anthony Gardner	£1m
Adam Virgo	Trainee	Stephen Kelly	Trainee
Kerry Mayo	Trainee	Reto Ziegler	Undisclosed
Richard Carpenter	Free transfer	Pedro Mendes	£2m
Charlie Oatway	£10,000*	Michael Carrick	£2.75m
Dan Harding	Trainee	Michael Brown	£500,000
Leon Knight	£50,000	Robbie Keane	£7m
Gary Hart	£1,000	Jermain Defoe	£7m
	(plus a set of kit)		

* Oatway came to the club in a £30,000 joint deal that also included defender Paul Watson from Brentford in 1999.

Liverpool bogey

Liverpool players and fans must have hated the sight of Albion in the 1980s, when the Seagulls held an Indian sign over the Merseyside club in both the league and FA Cup. From 1981/82 through to 1983/84, Liverpool were league champions, but over the three seasons they won just once in six meetings with Albion. A 3-3 draw at the Goldstone was followed by a 1-0 Albion win at Anfield (courtesy of an Andy Ritchie goal) in 1982/83 season. Liverpool won 3-1 at Anfield in October 1982, before Albion were drawn away to Liverpool in the fifth round of the FA Cup. On 20 February 1983, Albion recorded a historic 2-1 win, thanks to goals from Gerry Ryan and Jimmy Case. A month later, they drew 2-2 with Liverpool in the league at the Goldstone Ground. The following season, Albion – by now relegated to Division Two – were pitched against Liverpool in the FA Cup, this time at home in the fourth round. The match was screened live on ITV, and a nationwide audience saw Albion record another giant killing and win 2-0. Again, Gerry Ryan was a scorer; Terry Connor got the other. Liverpool ended Albion's dominance in a fairly emphatic style in a Milk Cup tie in 1985/86 when they hammered Albion 4-0 at Anfield on 20 October. The complete record is as follows:

Albion v Liverpool 1981-84

17 October 1981	Albion 3 Liverpool 3	Football League Division One
6 March 1982	Liverpool 0 Albion 1	Football League Division One
30 October 1982	Liverpool 3 Albion 1	Football League Division One
20 February 1983	Liverpool 1 Albion 2	FA Cup fifth round
22 March 1983	Albion 2 Liverpool 2	Football League Division One
29 January 1984	Albion 2 Liverpool 0	FA Cup fourth round

Old boy returns to haunt Albion

Hove-born Colin Woffinden played four games for Albion and scored one goal during the 1970s, but it is for two other Goldstone appearances that he appears in these pages. He made his Albion appearances during a six-month trial with the Seagulls during the 1970/71 season, but manager Pat Saward opted not to sign the forward, who had excelled in the non-league scene with Worthing, Eastbourne United and Lewes. Woffinden went on to play for Sutton United, Walton & Hersham and Leatherhead, and it was while he was with those last two clubs that he helped produce two of the biggest FA Cup shock defeats in the Albion's history – in consecutive seasons. In 1973/74, Isthmian League club Walton & Hersham were drawn at home to Albion in the first round of the FA Cup. With 6,500 fans packed into their rickety Stompond Lane ground for the first match on 24 November 1973, they held their league opponents to a goalless draw. The public expected Albion to ease through to the second round via the Goldstone replay, but it wasn't to be – four days later, the amateurs thrashed Albion 4-0 on their own ground. By the following season, Woffinden was on the books of Leatherhead, also of the Isthmian League. Again in the FA

Cup, Leatherhead were drawn to face Albion, this time in the third round of the competition. Peter Taylor's team had swept aside Aldershot and Brentford at the Goldstone Ground in rounds one and two, and Leatherhead were seen as an easy passage to round four. Again, it wasn't to be, and a 20,941-strong crowd witnessed Albion get beaten by a goal from Chris Kelly (nicknamed the Leatherhead Lip, and who became a national icon after his exploits). Leatherhead went on to give First Division Leicester City a real fright in the fourth round; they led 2-0 at Filbert Street, but the Foxes fought back to win the tie 3-2.

On loan for a day

Centre forward Chris Iwelumo spent just one day on loan with Albion before sealing a permanent switch from Stoke City. Albion were playing an away fixture at Chesterfield on 16 March 2004, and the Scottish-born striker first linked up with his team-mates at the team hotel on the same day. A transfer had been agreed between the two clubs and the player, but Football League regulations stipulated that in order for a permanent player to be eligible to play, they had to be signed by midday on the day preceding the match. With this deadline passed, Albion spotted a loophole in the regulations: loan signings could be made up until three hours before kick off. In a frantic hurry, the necessary documentation was faxed through to the team hotel, and Iwelumo put pen to paper on a loan transfer from Stoke at 4.30pm – three hours and 15 minutes before the evening kick-off. It all proved worth it, as Iwelumo scored Albion's second goal in a 2-0 win. The following day, he signed the permanent transfer from Stoke City to Albion, which annulled the loan arrangement.

Badges of distinction

Albion have been associated with several different styles of crests. Until 1970, the twin-town crests of Brighton and Hove had been used sporadically on the shirt. From January 2001 until May 2002, an updated version of the crests of the two towns – now brought together as a city – was used for the club's centenary shirt. In 1958/59, a shield with simple calligraphic writing spelling out the club's initials, BHAFC, adorned the shirt. The club adopted the 'Dolphins' nickname in 1969, but it wasn't until 1974 that the round badge with the club name, an image of a dolphin and the nickname was introduced. This was used on the programme but never worn on the club's shirts. The round seagull crest was first used in 1977 when the club changed their nickname from the Dolphins after fans adopted the 'Seagulls! Seagulls!' chant in response to rivals Crystal Palace's chants of 'Eagles!'. The crest was updated to reflect a new era in the club's history in 1998, shortly after Dick Knight took over as chairman.

Record transfer fees paid I

At £200, George Holley became Albion's record signing when he joined the club from Sunderland in July 1919. Signed by Charlie Webb shortly after he took over as manager, Holley arrived with a superb reputation, 10 England caps and a Football League championship medal to his name. The former England international pulled in the crowds, but he was considered past his best and only made 13 appearances for Albion, scoring five times, as a leg injury brought his career to a close. In February of the following year Albion also paid £200, this time to Luton Town, for the services of Dave Williams. It could hardly be considered money well spent as he left on a free transfer in May 1921 to join Maidstone United, then of the Kent League. Albion broke the £200 record when they signed defender Harry Bentley from Sheffield Wednesday in May 1920 for £250. That was money well spent, as he made 70 appearances for the club over the next two seasons. That record was broken in August 1921 when outside-right Freddie Groves joined from Arsenal for £500 and gave good service over three seasons, totalling 60 appearances and two goals. The record was set again in March 1925, when Albion paid West Ham United £650 for well-known centre forward Sam Jennings (who'd once attracted a £2250 fee when moving from Norwich City to Middlesbrough). Jennings proved a terrific buy, scoring more than a goal every other game with 63 goals in 115 games. The economic depression of the late 1920s and 1930s and the Second World War from 1939 to 1945 meant the £650 record stood for 23 years until February 1948, when Albion made their first four-figure signing (see 'Record transfer fees paid II', page 82).

Record defeats

Albion's all-time record defeat was, and remains, an 18-0 drubbing by Norwich City on Christmas Day 1940 (see 'An unhappy Christmas', page 63). Albion also lost 10-0 and 10-1 to Crystal Palace in wartime matches, in 1940 and 1942 respectively. Because these defeats happened in wartime, most books refer to Albion's 9-0 reverse at Middlesbrough in their first ever Second Division fixture as their record defeat. An 8-2 defeat to Bristol Rovers at the Goldstone Ground on 1 December 1973 (which, unfortunately for Albion, was featured on ITV's Big Match programme) is the club's heaviest home defeat.

Signing sensation

When Albion signed former England centre forward and double-winner Bobby Smith from Tottenham Hotspur in May 1964, the transfer made headline news. It was a major coup for Fourth Division Albion and then-boss Archie Macaulay. He had lured a player to the Goldstone Ground who just six months earlier had won the last of his 15 England caps in an 8-3 Wembley win over Northern Ireland. Smith also had a pretty impressive scoring record of 13 goals for England. He had started in the professional game with Chelsea, scoring 30 goals in 86 games before moving to Spurs in December 1955. At White Hart Lane, Smith scored 208 goals in all competitions. His 28 league strikes in 1960/61 helped Spurs win the first Football League and FA Cup double of the 20th century, and he also scored a goal in their 2-0 Cup Final win over Leicester City. In 1964, local Brighton bookmaker George Gunn paved the way for Smith's arrival – legend has it he paid off regular punter Smith's gambling debts. His first season at Albion was an unmitigated success as he hit 20 goals in 33 matches (he missed the other 15 through injury) and Albion won the Fourth Division championship.

What's in a name I

Brighton & Hove Albion are the only current Football League club with a name that consists of four words, although Bournemouth were once known as Bournemouth & Boscombe Athletic. At 21 letters, however, Albion's is the second-longest name, beaten only by Wolverhampton Wanderers.

Gory years

While the late 1970s are often referred to as the 'Glory Years' in Albion's history, many fans refer to the mid- to late-1990s as the 'Gory Years' or 'War Years'. It all began in July 1995 when Albion were in the Second Division. Under the headline 'Seagulls Migrate', the local paper, *The Argus*, broke the news that the board of directors (led by Bill Archer, Greg Stanley and David Bellotti) had sold the Goldstone Ground to retail and property development company Chartwell, and planned to enter into a ground-sharing arrangement with Portsmouth to use Fratton Park for home matches. The club were cagey about making a formal announcement but eventually admitted in a press release that Albion were due to move out at the end of the 1995/96 season. The release also announced plans for a 30,000-seat stadium on land at Waterhall, north of the A27 Brighton by-pass, in spite of a council remit not to sanction any developments north of the road. The news was greeted with stunned disbelief, but the fans soon began organising protests, which were to become a regular feature for the next couple of seasons. By the time of the final home match of the 1995/96 season, and with Albion already relegated to the bottom division of the Football League, the club had been offered a 12-month stay of execution. They could rent the Goldstone back for a further year at the cost of £480,000. Ahead of the match with York City, however, no decision was announced as the reviled directors played the risky game of trying to force the price down with brinkmanship. Desperate to save their club, supporters invaded the pitch and tore down the goalposts to force an abandonment and ensure they received maximum exposure for the club's plight. (Previously, only two domestic games in England had been abandoned because of supporters' interference.) The following day, Liam Brady, who had quit as manager earlier in the season, emerged as part of a consortium (which also included Dick Knight) wanting to buy out Archer, Stanley and Bellotti but, despite enormous fan pressure, the trio refused to budge. The following week, however, they announced they had reached an agreement to rent back the Goldstone from Chartwell for an undisclosed amount (believed by many to be the original asking price of £480,000). The stay of execution was exactly that, and little changed the following season. More protests and more pitch invasions followed, attracting a two-point deduction after the home match with Lincoln City was held up. Protests also included a walkout at the home game with Darlington, a boycott of the game against Mansfield Town, a march on chairman Archer's Lancashire home following an away fixture at Wigan and the unforgettable Fans United Day (see 'Fans United', page 92). The day before Albion's last ever match at the Goldstone Ground, Knight was announced as the new 'chairman-elect' of Brighton & Hove Albion. This was the penultimate match of the season, and Albion had to win to have any chance of avoiding relegation. The team completed the job a week later with a draw at Hereford (see 'Do or die day at Hereford', page 35). The off-pitch saga continued through the summer months, and it wasn't until 3 September 1997 that Knight eventually became chairman. The club had survived against all the odds, thanks largely to the efforts of the fans and the new chairman, but Knight now had to begin the massive task of rebuilding the Albion – and more importantly, finding the club a home in Sussex.

Floodlights at the Goldstone

Albion were one of the last football league clubs to install floodlights, largely because the club's manager at the time, Billy Lane, was opposed to his team playing night matches. The club eventually installed floodlights at the Goldstone Ground in

1960/61 and the first match under new lights was a friendly against Boldklubben Frem of Copenhagen on 10 April 1961. A crowd of 7,541 saw Albion run out 3-1 winners over the nine-times champions of Denmark. The final match under lights at the Goldstone was a Football League Division Three match against Barnet on 1 April 1997, which Albion won 1-0 thanks to a goal from forward Ian Baird.

Albion's last Christmas Day match

Albion's last ever Christmas Day match was a 2-2 draw against Swindon Town in the 1957/58 season. The tradition had begun in the early 1900s and was popular in the first half of the 20th century, attracting large holiday crowds. In those days, it was often the case that the two teams would play the return fixture on Boxing Day, so both clubs could take advantage of the winter holiday and enjoy a bumper crowd. By the 1950s the Christmas Day fixture wasn't proving as popular, however, particularly with the players. From 1958, clubs played only on Boxing Day and, for the next few seasons, this was closely followed by the return fixture for the two teams. For the record, Albert Mundy and Dave Sexton were Albion's scorers against Swindon Town that day, the last to score for the club on 25 December.

It's in the stars

A survey was once carried out into how likely a person was to become a professional footballer, depending on which month they were born in. To make the current Brighton & Hove Albion squad, it would appear that if you're born in September or October, there's much more chance of you getting signed up than if you were born in February. Seven of Albion's first-team squad were born in September and five in October, while not one of the players were born in February. When it comes to star signs, Virgo (seven instances) and Libra (five) are the most frequent amongst Albion players. Albion's current squad are no different from many of us, partaking in the traditional birthday cake and bun-fest, but twice this season the players can expect a double dose, as four members of the squad share birthdays. Gary Hart and Kerry Mayo were born exactly one year apart, on 21 September, while Jake Robinson was born on 23 October 1986, the day Albert Jarrett celebrated his second birthday. As the list below shows, Dean Hammond and John Sullivan's birthdays are one day apart, and the same is true of Paul Reid and Alex Revell.

Players' dates of birth

Current squad*	Birthday	Star sign
Wes Fogden	12 April 1988	Aries
Chris Breach	19 April 1986	Aries
Alex Frutos	23 April 1982	Taurus
Sam Rents	22 June 1987	Gemini
Michel Kuipers	26 June 1974	Cancer
Paul Reid	6 July 1979	Cancer
Alex Revell	7 July 1983	Cancer
Maheta Molango	24 July 1982	Leo
Dean Cox	12 August 1987	Leo
Colin Kazim-Richards	26 August 1986	Virgo
Richard Martin	1 September 1987	Virgo
Tommy Elphick	7 September 1987	Virgo
Adam El-Abd	11 September 1984	Virgo
Wayne Henderson	16 September 1983	Virgo
Kerry Mayo	21 September 1977	Virgo
Gary Hart	21 September 1976	Virgo
Richard Carpenter	30 September 1972	Libra
Joel Lynch	3 October 1987	Libra
Paul Hinshelwood	11 October 1987	Libra
Albert Jarrett	23 October 1984	Libra
Jake Robinson	23 October 1986	Libra
Guy Butters	30 October 1969	Scorpio
Joe Gatting	25 November 1987	Sagittarius
Charlie Oatway	28 November 1973	Sagittarius
Tommy Fraser	5 December 1987	Sagittarius
Doug Loft	25 December 1986	Capricorn
Adam Hinshelwood	8 January 1984	Capricorn
Scott Chamberlain	5 January 1988	Capricorn
Dean Hammond	7 March 1983	Pisces
John Sullivan	8 March 1988	Pisces

* As at 5 August 2006.

Young guns

With the exception of wartime football (during which juniors Reg Bowles (15), Stan Willemse (16), Charlie Chase (16) and John Collins (16) all played for Albion's first team), Albion fans had to wait until the late 1980s to cheer the first player under the age of 17 to appear in the first team. Ian Chapman became the first 16-year-old to play for the club in peacetime when he made his Albion debut in a Second Division fixture at Birmingham City on Valentine's Day 1987, aged 16 years and 259 days. (Albion lost the game 2-0.) The Brighton-born left-back made five further appearances before his 17th birthday and went on to give excellent service during a 10-year, 331-game spell with the club. Chapman's record was surpassed by Simon Fox, who was 16 years and 238 days when he made the first of 24 appearances as a substitute when Albion beat Fulham 2-0 at the Goldstone on 23 April 1994. Ten days short of his 17th birthday, Jake Robinson became Albion's youngest ever scorer when he hit the second goal in a 2-0 win over Forest Green in the Football League Trophy first round tie at Withdean Stadium. His goal beat Mick Conway's record; he had scored on his Albion debut in a Division Two fixture against Nottingham Forest on 28 April 1973, aged 17 years and 48 days. Conway also held the record of Albion's youngest ever league debutant until Chapman played against Birmingham in 1987.

An exhausting season

These days, most clubs play approximately 50 games (more if they're successful in the cups and European competition) between early August and May. In the 1912/13 season, Albion played 63 matches in the Southern League Division One, Southern Alliance, FA Cup and Southern Charity Cup. They crammed the games in, from the moment they kicked off with a 2-0 win over Portsmouth on 4 September to their final match, a 2-2 draw with Millwall at home on 30 April. The Albion's success in the Charity Cup was one of the reasons for the mammoth season. They reached the final, where they lost 4-1 to Queen's Park Rangers at Millwall's Cold Blow Lane Ground. Perhaps it was no surprise that Albion were defeated – they'd had to squeeze in an exhausting seven matches in 15 days. The largest number of Albion games in a post-war season came in 1992/93 when they played 59 fixtures – 46 Football League Division Two matches, five FA Cup ties, four League Cup ties and four Football League Trophy (then known as the Associate Members' Cup) matches. As for the individual record, central defender Norman Gall missed only the first game of the 1966/67 season before playing 57 times in one season – a club record. This feat has since been matched in the promotion season of 1987/88 when both central defender Keith Dublin and goalkeeper John Keeley played in every league and cup match. Three seasons later, Dean Wilkins was ever-present for 57 matches as Albion reached the Division Two Play-Off Final.

Eleven matches without a change

When Albion manager Charlie Webb named the team for Albion's Division Three South encounter with Coventry City on 17 November 1934 (which Albion won 2-0), little did he realise that he would name the same team for the next 10 fixtures against Folkestone (FAC, 3-1), Gillingham (0-0), Queen's Park Rangers (FAC, 2-1), Bristol City (0-1), Millwall, Luton Town (0-4), Luton Town again (4-1), Bristol Rovers (0-0), Charlton Athletic (2-1) and, finally, an historic FA Cup third round meeting with Football League champions Arsenal, which Albion lost 2-0. The line-up would have been an easy one for fans to remember as it included four of the most common surnames of the era: Brown, Smith, Jones and Wilson. In full, the team was: Charlie Thomson, Ernie King, Herbert Jones, Len Darling, Paul Mooney, Dave Walker, Bert Jepson, Bobby Farrell, Oliver Brown, Potter Smith, Tug Wilson.

Consecutive appearances

Albion goalkeeper Eric Gill holds one record that is extremely unlikely to ever be beaten. The veteran of 296 appearances made an astonishing 247 of them in succession. Between 21 February 1953, when he kept a clean sheet at Reading, and 1 March 1958, when illness cruelly ruled him out of the away match at Coventry City, he played every single first-team match. The record beat the previous best of goalkeeper Billy Hayes, who had played 175 games between 2 October 1920 and 3 May 1924. The first outfield player to surpass 100 games was right-half Billy Booth, who began a 143 game sequence when he played in 28 October 1908 by scoring in a 2-0 win over Luton Town at the Goldstone Ground. Winger Peter O'Sullivan (second in the club's all-time list of appearances with 491 senior appearances) holds the record for the most number of consecutive games for an outfield player. He made the first of 194 successive appearances at Torquay United on 16 October 1970 and the last at Charlton Athletic on 24 September 1974, when he was dropped and made available for transfer by manager Peter Taylor. 'Sully' wasn't out of the team for long, and after missing only seven matches he went on to complete every minute of the remaining 34 matches of the season.

Albion at the World Cup

Only three players have ever played in the World Cup Finals while on Albion's books. Steve Foster played in England's 1-0 win over Kuwait in Bilbao on 25 June in the 1982 World Cup. Sammy Nelson appeared for Northern Ireland on the day they beat hosts Spain 1-0 in Valencia. Nelson also appeared in Northern Ireland's match with Austria on 1 July in Madrid. Four years later, Steve Penney was part of the Northern Ireland squad in Mexico for the 1986 World Cup Finals. The Albion winger played in the 1-1 draw with Algeria on 3 June and in the 2-1 defeat to Spain four days later – both games were played in Guadalajara.

Record goal-getter

Albion's all-time leading scorer is Bert Stephens. He scored a phenomenal 174 goals in 366 appearances between 1935 and 1948. He scored 87 of his goals in wartime football, but when you consider that the son of Kent was effectively a left-winger (known as an outside-left in the 1930s) and was never Albion's penalty-taker, the feat is even more amazing. Stephens was top scorer in four separate seasons and is one of only two Albion strikers to have hit 20-plus goals in three consecutive seasons (Albert Mundy 1954/55 to 1956/57 is the other). His total included six hat-tricks. Only two other players topped the 100-goal mark: Tommy Cook with 123 strikes in 209 games (and an impressive 0.59 goals per Albion game) between 1921 and 1929; and Jock Davie, who scored three less than Cook in 191 games (an even more impressive average of 0.63 goals per game). Kit Napier, Albion's top scorer for five seasons out of six between 1966/67 and 1971/72, can be considered unlucky not to have reached three figures. He ended on 99 goals before leaving Albion for Blackburn Rovers in August 1972 after a fall out with Pat Saward.

Biggest crowd

The biggest crowd ever to watch Albion was 100,000 at Wembley Stadium for the 1983 FA Cup Final against Manchester United on 21 May 1983. The biggest crowd at the Goldstone Ground was the attendance of 36,747 for the Second Division match with Fulham on 27 December 1958, which yielded gate receipts of £4376. Albion didn't disappoint as they produced their best performance of the season to beat the eventual Division Two runners-up 3-0, with two goals from Tommy Dixon and one from Adrian Thorne. The biggest crowd to watch Albion play a 'home' match at Gillingham's Priestfield Stadium were the 6339 fans who turned up for the bottom-of-the-table clash with Doncaster Rovers on 14 February 1998. The match was billed as 'Fans United II: The heart of football' (see 'Fans United', page 92) as a protest against the troubles then engulfing the two clubs. Albion had removed the reviled regime that had sold the Goldstone but the rebuilding process was long and arduous, while Doncaster fans were suffering at the hands of owner Ken Richardson, who had tried to burn down the club's main stadium in order to make a fraudulent insurance claim, and was now refusing to sell the club. On this occasion the teams did disappoint (if the fans didn't). Neither mustered a shoot on target and the match was a dire goalless draw. Albion's biggest crowd at Withdean Stadium so far (as at the start of the 2006/07 season) was 7999 for the championship match with Southampton on Saturday 8 April. The match finished in a 2-0 defeat for Albion, headed for relegation to League One.

Four monthly awards

Pat Saward and Alan Mullery hold the club record for Manager of the Month Awards. Saward won the award four times between April 1971 and March 1973. Mullery matched that feat between September 1976 (when he won the award for the entire league) and December 1978. Micky Adams won Manager of the Month Awards three times. Chris Cattlin, Barry Lloyd and Liam Brady each won two.

Newcastle clincher

Albion clinched promotion to the First Division for the first – and to date, only – time in their history with a convincing 3-1 win at Newcastle United on 5 May 1979. The Seagulls, wearing their all-yellow away strip, were cheered on by somewhere between 7,000 and 10,000 travelling Albion supporters who packed the Leazes End at St James's Park, and saw goals from Brian Horton, Peter Ward and Gerry Ryan put them 3-0 in front at the interval. In the dressing room, the players were stunned when manager Alan Mullery began ranting and raving, tearing them off a strip for their first-half display – it was put down to nerves. It took an interjection from Brian Horton to calm the Albion manager. Some 45 minutes later, despite a consolation for the Magpies, scored by Alan Shoulder, Albion had won the match and all the nerves had evaporated. Chairman Mike Bamber embraced Mullery on a pitch that was swamped by Albion fans. The following day, more than 100,000 people turned out on the streets of Brighton & Hove to cheer the achievements of the team, and some 25,000 packed the Goldstone Ground as the team did a lap of honour prior to a four-mile open-top bus tour to a reception at Hove Town Hall. The team on that historic day at Newcastle was: Eric Steele; Chris Cattlin, Andy Rollings, Paul Clark, Gary Williams; Gerry Ryan (Malcolm Poskett), Brian Horton, Peter Sayer, Peter O'Sullivan; Peter Ward, Teddy Maybank.

Most goals in a match

Two players have scored six goals in a single match for Albion, but both in extenuating circumstances. Legendary Albion goal-scorer Arthur Attwood managed six in the club's 12-0 win over Sussex amateurs Shoreham in the FA Cup first qualifying round match at the Goldstone Ground on 1 October 1932. Albion had entered in the qualifying stages of the competition after a cock-up by the club secretary (see 'FA Cup records', page 53). Don Welsh – later to become Albion manager in 1948 – also hit six for Albion. Welsh's goals came in a thrilling 7-4 home win over Luton Town, but he was appearing as a guest player in a wartime fixture. Four Albion players have managed five goals in one game. Jock Davie did it in an 8-2 win over Chelsea in a wartime fixture at the Goldstone on 31 January 1942, and Frank Scott in a Southern League Division Two match at Southall on 28 February 1903. Jack Doran and Adrian Thorne both achieved the feat in Football League Division Three South matches. Doran produced fireworks in a 7-0 win over Northampton Town on 5 November 1921 (seven days later, Albion lost the return fixture 2-0 at Northampton). Thorne gained legendary status among Albion supporters when he hit his quintet of goals at the most opportune time, in a promotion-clinching 6-0 win over Watford at the Goldstone Ground on 30 April 1958.

Olympics, England and Spurs at the Goldstone

The Goldstone Ground was used for a variety of non-Albion matches over many years, including England amateur internationals and the Sussex Senior Cup Final, until 1997, when the bulldozers moved in. Perhaps the most notable of these non-Albion matches came on 26 July 1948 when Afghanistan met Luxembourg in an Olympic Games football match. Press reports of the day suggested the Afghans would play the fixture in bare feet but they didn't, much to the disappointment of the 7,000 crowd. The Football Association used the Goldstone Ground on two occasions. The first was for an under-21 international against Norway on 6 September 1977, in which Albion's Peter Ward scored a hat-trick in a 6-0 win. The other was on 14 November 1989 for an England B international against Italy, in which an England side that included Paul Gascoigne drew 1-1. The ground also hosted four Intertoto Cup matches in the summer of 1995, two involving Tottenham Hotspur and two involving Wimbledon – neither could use their usual home stadiums due to redevelopment work. A Spurs side made up largely of youth and loan players played the first fixture against Swiss side Lucerne on 25 June, which ended in a 2-0 defeat. The second match (Spurs' third of the competition) was on 15 July against Swedish Osters IF, which Spurs lost 2-1. Wimbledon didn't fare much better. They lost 4-0 to Turkish side Bursaspor Kulubu on 24 June and drew 0-0 with Israeli outfit Beitar Jerusalem on 15 July.

Million-pound men

Only two players have ever commanded £1m-plus transfer fees on leaving Albion. Striker Bobby Zamora moved to Spurs in a £1.5m deal in July 2003, while Adam Virgo moved to Celtic for a fee of £1.5m in July 2005. Gareth Barry (see 'Transfer tribunal', page 65) eventually cost Aston Villa over £1m, but his initial fee on leaving the Goldstone was just £3250.

FA Cup records

Brighton & Hove Albion became the first club to have played in every round (qualifying and proper) of the English FA Cup competition, when they reached the FA Cup Final in 1983. Albion also set the record for the most FA Cup games in one season. It was all down to an administrative error by the club secretary, Albert Underwood, in 1932. In the build up to the 1932/33 season, Underwood forgot to claim exemption from the qualifying rounds and Albion were forced to enter the competition in the first qualifying round. The club did consider not entering at all, but bowed to pressure from supporters and kicked off with a 12-0 win over Shoreham at the Goldstone. Qualifying matches against Worthing, Hastings and Barnet followed, before Albion beat Crystal Palace, Wrexham (after a replay), First Division Chelsea (also after a replay) and Bradford Park Avenue. A then-record Goldstone crowd of 32,310 saw Albion knocked out 3-2 by First Division West Ham in the sixth round, in their 11th FA Cup match of the season. Nottingham Forest equalled this record run of matches when they were runners-up in the competition in 1991, while three years previously Wimbledon matched Albion's feat of playing in every round.

England captains say hello and farewell

England captain Kevin Keegan played his last ever senior game, for Newcastle United, against Albion at St James's Park on 12 May 1984, and the future England manager was on the score-sheet as the Magpies won 3-1. England captain David Beckham played his first ever senior game for Manchester United against Albion at the Goldstone on 23 October 1992 in a League Cup second round first-leg match. Danny Wallace opened the scoring for Manchester United in the first half, but Matthew Edwards equalised for Albion, just seconds after Beckham had come on as a substitute, to earn a 1-1 draw.

England keeper's landmark comes against Albion

A crowd of 7944 flocked to Brisbane Road to see England goalkeeper Peter Shilton play his 1000th league game against Albion for Leyton Orient on 22 December 1996. The veteran keeper, who had also played for Leicester City, Nottingham Forest, Southampton and Bolton Wanderers, and had won a record 125 caps for England, hardly got his gloves dirty in what was probably the easiest 90 minutes of his career, as a lacklustre Albion side failed to muster a single shot on target and went down 2-0.

Player of the Season awards

John Napier became Albion's first ever winner of Player of the Season, at the end of the 1968/69 season. The centre-half was ever present, and scored twice for Albion as they finished 12th in the Third Division. Paul McShane became the first loan player to win the award, in 2004/05. The young defender was on loan from Manchester United for much of the season and played 40 games for Albion, scoring four goals. Danny Cullip, Steve Foster and Bobby Zamora each won the award twice. The complete list of winners is as follows:

1968/69	John Napier	1987/88	Garry Nelson
1969/70	Stewart Henderson	1988/89	John Keeley
1970/71	Norman Gall	1989/90	Keith Dublin
1971/72	Bert Murray	1990/91	Perry Digweed
1972/73	Eddie Spearritt	1991/92	Mark Gall
1973/74	Norman Gall	1992/93	Steve Foster
1974/75	not chosen	1993/94	Kurt Nogan
1975/76	not chosen	1994/95	Peter Smith
1976/77	Brian Horton	1995/96	Ian Chapman
1977/78	Peter O'Sullivan	1996/97	not chosen
1978/79	Mark Lawrenson	1997/98	Jeff Minton
1979/80	Steve Foster	1998/99	Gary Hart
1980/81	Michael Robinson	1999/2000	Danny Cullip
1981/82	Andy Ritchie	2000/01	Bobby Zamora
1982/83	Gary Stevens	2001/02	Bobby Zamora
1983/84	Jimmy Case	2002/03	Danny Cullip
1984/85	Graham Moseley	2003/04	Guy Butters
1985/86	Dean Saunders	2004/05	Adam Virgo
1986/87	Terry Connor	2005/06	Paul McShane

We've never beaten Chelsea in the league

At the start of the 2006/07 season, the only Premiership and Football League teams Albion had never beaten in a league encounter were Accrington Stanley, Boston United, Chelsea and Yeovil Town. There is a fair excuse when it comes to Accrington, Boston and Yeovil, in that they have never met Albion in a Football League encounter – indeed, Albion have never played Accrington.

But in Albion's four league clashes with Chelsea, the West London side have a 100% record. Albion have beaten three of the teams in the FA Cup, however – Chelsea in the FA Cup in 1933, Yeovil in the FA Cup in 1952 and Boston in the Football League Trophy in 2003. Albion also beat Chelsea during the Second World War.

Siblings I

The following 10 sets of siblings had appeared for Albion as at the end of 2005/06 season:

The Browns: Irvin, Alan and Stan
The Buckleys: Frank and Chris
The Burtenshaws: Steve and Charlie
The Easthams: George and Harry
The Elphicks: Gary and Tommy
The Fox's: Mark and Simon
The Longstaffs: Bert and Harvey
The Rutherfords: Jack and Jim
The Virgos: James and Adam
The Wilsons: Joe and Glen

Not all of them have played together. The three Brown brothers (see 'Siblings II', page 60) never played in the same team. Charlie Burtenshaw only played wartime football for Albion (as did George and Harry Eastham) but Steve Burtenshaw played 252 senior matches between 1951 and 1967. The Elphicks never appeared together. Gary did play in the same match in which brother Tommy made his debut at Reading in December 2005, but Gary had been sent off by the time Tommy came onto the pitch as a substitute. James Virgo played two games between 1995 and 1997, while brother Adam didn't make his senior debut for Albion until 2001. Joe and Glen Wilson (see 'Siblings III', page 77) are the pair of brothers who made the most appearances for Albion – they played 353 and 436 games respectively – but in not one of them were they together in the same side. Of those who did play at the same time, Frank and Chris Buckley appeared together for Albion 22 times in the 1905/06 season (in the 1930s Frank became one of the game's most-respected managers while with Wolverhampton Wanderers). The Longstaffs played seven games together in 1912/13, but Bert's 443 appearances (and 86 goals) shadowed brother Harvey's total of four goals in nine games. Centre-back Jack and left-back Jim Rutherford both spent one season with Albion in 1920/21 – the club's first in the Football League – and each made 29 senior appearances, 15 of which were together. The Foxes became the first brothers to play for the Albion at the same time since the Rutherfords, when they played at York City in March 1995. Mark appeared 26 times (scoring once) and Simon 24, with five of those appearances being together. Paul Hinshelwood signed professional in June 2006 and will hope to follow in the footsteps of his brother Adam, who made his Albion debut in a 3-1 win at Burnley on 10 August 2002. Fred and Jack Eacock both played for Albion (1919/20 and 1908/10 respectively). It is known they were both from the same family, but the exact relationship isn't clear; however, it is suspected they were cousins rather than brothers.

Biggest name in football

Micky Adams persuaded the biggest name in English football to sign for the Seagulls in the summer of 1999. Midfielder Anthony Philip David Terry Frank Donald Stanley Gerry Gordon Stephen James Oatway (better known to Albion fans as Charlie) boasted the longest name of any professional footballer when he signed for Albion from Brenford. The story behind his 11 forenames was that Oatway's father was a keen Queen's Park Rangers fan and named his son, born on 28 November 1973, after Rangers' 1973 first-team line up. When his parents told his aunt the proposed name, she said, 'He'll look a right Charlie,' and the name stuck.

Foxes connection

No fewer than five Albion managers have also been in the employ of Leicester City (or Leicester Fosse, as they were once known). John Jackson, the original manager of Brighton & Hove Albion, had been a trainer with Leicester Fosse. More recently, Micky Adams left Albion in October 2001 to become assistant manager to Dave Bassett at Leicester; he later became manager when Bassett became Director of Football. The man who replaced Adams at Albion was Peter Taylor, whose sacking by Leicester had created the opportunity for Bassett and Adams. Scot Mark McGhee was boss of the Foxes from December 1994 to December 1995. Albion's legendary manager of the 1950s, Billy Lane, also had a Leicester connection. He played for the club in the 1920s.

Youngest skipper

Ronnie Welch became Albion's youngest ever captain in February 1974 when he took the skipper's armband aged 21 years and 143 days. Second youngest was Bobby Zamora who captained Albion just the once, at Sheffield United on 19 October 2002, aged 21 years and 276 days. John Napier was also an Albion skipper at 21, while Adam Hinshelwood, Leon Knight and Ian Goodwin all captained Albion at the tender age of 22.

Wolves' bogey side

Albion were unwelcome visitors in Wolverhampton for many years, because the club boasted a spectacular 100% record over Wolves in Football League fixtures until the 1991/92 season. It became an 85.7% record on 18 December 1991, when Wolves completed a 2-0 victory. Prior to that, the Seagulls had been victorious on their six previous visits to Molineux. The club's first ever trip to the ground was for a First Division fixture on 21 December 1979, which Albion won 3-1. Subsequent victories followed (2-0, 1-0, 1-0, 4-2 and 3-2) before the 2-0 reverse in 1991. Wolves' away record against Albion in Sussex makes equally wretched reading for the West Midlands. They never won a league match at the Goldstone Ground, although they did win a League Cup third round tie in 1969 and an FA Cup third round tie 10 years later (both ended in 3-2 successes). Wanderers' first ever league victory at Brighton was 1-0, courtesy of a Kenny Miller goal, at Withdean, on 14 September 2004.

UK top 40

Albion have been associated with a few hit records. The club released The Boys In The Old Brighton Blue on vinyl as their official FA Cup Final record in 1983 (the flip side was The Goldstone Rap). Another record from the same era was Where Seagulls Fly, but the most successful single was released by specially formed local band Seagulls Ska. Their club-backed record, We Want Falmer! was a reworking of the old Piranhas hit Tom Hark. The CD single (which included a ska version of Sussex By The Sea and the anti-Crystal Palace song Donkey Derby) reached number 17 in the official UK Top 40 in January 2005. The song's lyrics are as follows:

We want Falmer
We need Falmer
We need Falmer
We want Falmer (x2)

We Brighton fans are angry – we've been messed around
Since the wayward Archer sold the Goldstone Ground
We're stuck in an athletics track we really hate
Like playing in Albania Division Eight

CHORUS
The whole thing's daft
I don't know why
We have to laugh
Or else we'll cry
Our ground's too small
The costs too high
Without Falmer
Our club will die

For years the planning process has dragged on and on
A paralytic snail wouldn't take that long
So listen Mr Prescott as we tell you how
We need our Falmer stadium – we need it NOW!

CHORUS
The whole thing's daft
I don't know why
We have to laugh
Or else we'll cry
Our ground's too small
The costs too high
Without Falmer
Our club will die (x2)

We want Falmer
We need Falmer
We need Falmer
We want Falmer (x4 and fade)

Mayo on everything

Kerry Mayo is the only player to have featured for Albion in competitive fixtures at three different home grounds. He made his Albion League debut in a 3-1 defeat against Carlisle United at the Goldstone on 23 November 1996; played in Albion's first competitive home fixture during a two-year ground-share at Gillingham's Priestfield Stadium (a 1-1 draw with Leyton Orient in the League Cup first round, first leg) on 15 August 1997; and made his first senior appearance at Withdean in the 1-0 win over Hartlepool on 6 November 1990. In the early days of the club, several players appeared for Albion at Dyke Road Field (for early non-competitive fixtures), Sussex Cricket Club's County Ground and The Goldstone Ground.

Last hurrah

Albion's last ever game at the Goldstone took place on 26 April 1997 against Doncaster Rovers. A crowd of 11,341 saw Albion win a tense, tight game 1-0, thanks to Stuart Storer's 67th-minute goal. They also saw Albion striker Ian Baird sent off after 19 minutes, along with Doncaster's Darren Moore. The victory lifted Albion off the bottom of the Football League and maintained hopes of avoiding relegation to the Conference. Thousands invaded the pitch at the final whistle to collect souvenirs. The Albion line up on the day was: (4-4-2) Mark Ormerod; John Humphrey, Ross Johnson, Mark Morris, Stuart Tuck; Stuart Storer, Jeff Minton, Kerry Mayo, Paul McDonald (Robbie Reinelt); Ian Baird, Craig Maskell. Subs not used: Dave Martin, Gary Hobson.

Siblings II

No fewer than 10 sets of siblings have appeared for Albion, but the Brown brothers are the only trio of siblings to appear for the Seagulls, although none of the boys played at the same time. Irvin, Alan and Stan Brown were born in Lewes, but only Irvin and Alan came through junior ranks at the club. Irvin made three appearances in 1957/58, while Alan made eight appearances, scoring twice in 1961/62. Stan began his professional career with Fulham, signing forms in May 1959 and joined Albion on loan in 1972. He played 397 senior games for Fulham, the majority of them in the First Division. The Brown boys' cousin Gary, also born in Lewes, was another member of the family to play for Albion; he made one appearance for the club against Luton Town in a League Cup tie in September 1965.

Millenniummmm

Brighton-born Darren Freeman became the first English professional player to score in the new millennium. He achieved the feat by opening the scoring after the first two minutes of Albion's 4-2 win over Exeter at Withdean Stadium on 3 January 2000, and was presented with a bottle of champagne by TV presenter and Albion fan Des Lynam on behalf of then-league sponsors Nationwide.

Shortest career

Lasting just five minutes, goalkeeper Chris May's was the shortest professional career with Albion. The 19-year-old scholar replaced the injured Michel Kuipers in the 85th minute of a 0-0 draw with Nottingham Forest on 22 January 2005. He was released at the end of the 2004/05 season without being offered professional terms at the club. May's five-minute appearance beat the previous record of eight minutes, set by Sean Edwards. The Hastings-born full back replaced Chris Hutchings (injured) eight minutes from the end of a 3-1 victory over Crystal Palace in a Full Members Cup tie on 16 October 1985. Incidentally, Edwards' Albion career was the same length as Albion legend Peter Ward's England career; Ward came on as a sub for eight minutes in the match against Australia in May 1980. This is also a record for the shortest England career.

Unique hat trick

Steve Gatting is the only man to have appeared three times for Brighton & Hove Albion at Wembley Stadium. He played in the 1983 FA Cup Final and the 1983 final replay, after Albion drew the original game 2-2 with Manchester United, and he appeared for Albion in the 1991 Division Two play-off final against Notts County.

Tallest player

At 6ft 6ins, Florent Chaigneau is Albion's tallest player to date. The giant goalkeeper, an under-17 World Cup winner with France in

2001, spent the 2005/06 season on loan from French club Rennes. The tallest outfield players to represent Albion are Mark McCammon and Junior Lewis, both at 6ft 5ins.

Albion's tallest players

Florent Chaigneau	6ft 6ins
Mark McCammon	6ft 5ins
David Yelldell	6ft 5ins
Junior Lewis	6ft 5ins*
Juergen Sommer	6ft 4ins
Mark Beeney	6ft 4ins
Joe Corrigan	6ft 4ins
Rami Shabaan	6ft 4ins
Mark Walton	6ft 4ins
Dave Beasant	6ft 4ins

* Some sources incorrectly state Junior Lewis's height as only 6ft 2ins.

Penalty record

On Easter Monday, 27 March 1989, in the Second Division match between Crystal Palace and Albion, referee Kelvin Morton set a world record when he awarded five penalties – four of them to the home team. Palace missed three of the four. Alan Curbishley scored Albion's kick, but that didn't stop Palace winning the game 2-1.

England internationals

Just three men have been capped for England while in the employ of Brighton & Hove Albion – and England have won every game in which an Albion player has featured. Tommy Cook played against Wales in the Home International Championship at Swansea on 28 February 1925, when England won 2-1. Peter Ward came on as a substitute in the 2-1 win over Australia in Sydney on 31 May 1980. Steve Foster played three times for England, against Northern Ireland (4-0) and Holland (2-0), both at Wembley in the build up to the 1982 World Cup in Spain, and at the finals in the 1-0 win over Kuwait in Bilbao, meaning England never conceded with Foster at the heart of their defence.

First ever hard man

Albion's first ever hard man was captain and utility player Frank McAvoy. In December 1901, the fiery Scot argued with Albion manager John Jackson. The row simmered until it came to a head in February 1902, when McAvoy and team-mate Clem Barker visited Jackson's pub, the Farm Tavern. The Albion manager wasn't home, but McAvoy is alleged to have told Mrs Jackson, 'We're going to the station to meet your husband, and consider yourself lucky if he is brought home alive!'. A couple of weeks later at Hove Police Court, the pair were convicted of threatening behaviour, fined £10 and bound over to keep the peace. Unsurprisingly, neither man played for Albion again – McAvoy returned to his native Scotland via a season at Watford, and Barker returned to amateur football.

The old guard

Albion's oldest ever player was Sam Cowan, who became Albion's trainer in 1938 and was forced into action on three occasions during the Second World War. The last of these appearances came in a 3-0 defeat at Bournemouth on 13 October 1945, at the age of 44 years and 156 days. Albion's oldest peacetime player was former FA Cup winner and England goalkeeper Dave Beasant. The veteran stopper was the oldest player in the professional leagues at the time, and it was at the ripe old age of 44 years and 45 days that he made the last of his appearances for his 12th club in a 2-2 draw with Grimsby Town on 4 May 2003. The oldest outfield player to play for Albion in peacetime was midfielder Jimmy Case, who became the first over-40 to play for the club – he was 41 years and 166 days old when he played his final senior match at home to Swansea City on 31 October 1995. Player-coach Case eventually quit playing in November 1995 due to a bad neck injury sustained in a reserve match against Arsenal, and later that month, he stepped up to replace Liam Brady as manager.

An unhappy Christmas

Albion suffered their heaviest ever defeat on Christmas morning, 1940. A wartime team travelled to Norwich City on Christmas Eve, although 'team' is probably not the correct word in this instance. Manager Charlie Webb had only four players at his disposal – senior pro Joe Wilson and three juniors (teenager Roy Watts and 16-year-olds Charlie Chase and Charlie Harman). Bolton Wanderers defender Jimmy Ithell guested in defence. Norwich City junior players and Norfolk-based servicemen filled the remaining six places in the line-up. The home team won an easy 18-0 victory, which was the record score in wartime football. Little is known of Albion's goalkeeper on the day, although he is listed in several football history books as Mr A Bartram.

Roberts record

At the end of the 2003/04 season, Ben Roberts equalled the goalkeeping record of five consecutive clean sheets in successive Football League matches, but a career-ending injury prevented the goalkeeper from adding to his record. In all competitions, Roberts carried the run into a sixth game, the first leg of the end-of-season play-off semi-final against Swindon, but he conceded his first two goals in 632 minutes of football when Rory Fallon scored in the second leg of the tie at Withdean Stadium. Nonetheless, Albion eventually won through to the final on penalties, thanks to a Roberts save and Swindon miss in the shoot out, and the Bishop Auckland-born stopper made it seven clean sheets in eight matches by helping Albion to a 1-0 win over Bristol City in the final at the Millennium Stadium.

What's in a name II

Brighton & Hove Albion is the only current Football League club to be named after two towns. Brighton and Hove have now been brought together to become a city, but the club was originally named after the two separate seaside towns.

Scored with his first touch

Little was known of Peter Ward when he made his Albion and league debut at Hereford on 27 March 1976. Having been signed from Burton Albion in May 1975, he'd impressed in Albion's reserves and was handed his big chance by boss Peter Taylor, who played him up front in place of top scorer Fred Binney. The moved paid off, as Ward scored with his first touch after just 50 seconds. With the Match of the Day cameras at the game, Ward became a household name overnight. Maheta Molango achieved the same feat in the first game of the 2004/05 season in a 3-2 defeat at Reading.

Scored with his last touch

James Virgo is believed to be the only Albion player to have scored with his last touch in a professional game for the club. The Brighton-born left back made only two appearances for Albion, one as a substitute in a 2-0 League Cup defeat to Fulham at the Goldstone Ground in August 1995, the other, also against Fulham, in the Associate Members' Cup (then better known as the Auto Windscreens Shield) when he rifled a free kick to seal victory for Albion in golden goal extra time. He never appeared again.

Transfer tribunal

Gareth Barry, a schoolboy with Albion in the chaotic 1990s, earned the club over £1m after the FA ruled that Aston Villa should pay a great deal more than the £3250 they'd given Albion for him. The tribunal ruled they should pay a transfer fee of £150,000, appearance-related payments of £650,000, £25,000 for Barry's first England under-21 cap and £200,000 for his first senior cap. Aston Villa boss John Gregory, furious at the outcome, made a faux pas by claiming Seagulls chairman Dick Knight would not have recognised Barry if he was standing on Brighton Beach holding a football, with a Seagull on his head. That was unlikely, as Knight's nephew Michael Standing, an England youth international who moved from Brighton to Villa at the same time as Barry, was the young defender's best friend.

Record transfer fee received II

The first four-figure transfer fee Albion ever received was the £1500 (plus centre forward George Beech) that Sheffield Wednesday swapped for David Parkes in March 1914. That record was beaten 10 years later to the month, when Arsenal paid £3000 for club captain Andy Neil – a record that stood for 25 years. It was broken when Stan Willemse joined Chelsea for £6000 in July 1949.

Team colours

Albion's kit was unbranded between 1901 and the end of the 1974/75 season, but from the start of the following season it was made by sports clothing firm Umbro, and sported the company logo. Albion's first sponsor was airline British Caledonian in 1980. Others to have sponsored the club include Phoenix Brewery, Nobo (a visual display board manufacturer), TSB Bank, Sandtex (a paint manufacturer), Donatello (a Brighton-based Italian restaurant) and Skint Records. Donatello, main shirt sponsors in 1998/99, also became the club's first back-of-shirt and short sponsors in 2005/06. Albion's kit has been manufactured by a number of different suppliers, including Umbro, Bukta, Adidas, Admiral and Errea.

Albion's team colours 1901-2006

Era	Shirt colours	Short colours	Sponsor, supplier
2006-	Blue-and-white stripes, with blue back	White	(Skint, Errea)
2004-06	Light blue-and-white stripes	White	(Skint, Errea)
2002-04	Blue-and-white stripes	White	(Skint, Errea)
2001-02	Blue-and-white stripes*	White	(Skint, Errea)
1999-2000	Blue-and-white stripes	White	(Skint, Errea)
1998-99	Blue-and-white stripes	Blue	(Donatello, Super League)
1997-98	Broad central, plus additional narrow blue stripes	Blue	(Sandtex, Super League)
1994-97	Blue-and-white stripes	Blue	(Sandtex, Admiral)
1993-94	Blue-and-white pin-stripes, blue sleeves	Blue	(Sandtex, Ribero)
1991-93	Blue-and-white stripes	Blue-and-white stripes	(TSB, Ribero)

1989-91	Blue-and-white stripes, white sleeves	Blue	(NOBO, Sports Express)
1987-89	Blue-and-white stripes	Blue	(NOBO, Spall)
1986-87	Blue	White	(NOBO, Adidas)
1983-86	Blue	White	(Phoenix Brewery, Adidas)
1980-83	Blue	Blue	(British Caledonian, Adidas)
1977-80	Blue-and-white stripes, white sleeves	Blue	(Bukta)
1975-77	Blue-and-white stripes	Blue	(Umbro)
1974-75	White	White	
1972-74	Blue-and-white stripes	Blue	
1971-72	Blue-and-white stripes	Blue	
1970-71	White	White	
1964-70	Blue	White	
1963-64	Blue-and-white stripes	White	
1959-63	Blue-and-white stripes	White	
1958-59	Narrow blue stripes on white	White	
1951-58	Blue-and-white stripes	White	
1948-51	Blue, white sleeves and collars	White	
1914-48	Blue-and-white stripes	White	
1910-14	Blue-and-white stripes, blue collar	White	
1906-10	Blue-and-white stripes	White	
1905-06	Blue-and-white stripes, white collar	White	
1904-05	Blue-and-white stripes	White	
1901-04	Blue	White	

*A special shirt bearing the old town crests of Brighton and Hove was launched to commemorate the club's centenary on 1 January 2001, and worn until the end of the 2001/02 season.

Goldstone Ghosts

John Baine (aka Attila The Stockbroker), who would later become
the club's poet in residence, wrote the following poem to mark the
occasion of the Albion's last ever match at the Goldstone Ground,
on Saturday 26 April 1997.

As bulldozers close in upon our old, beloved home
and those who stand to profit rub their hands
so we gather here together in sad, angry disbelief
and for one last time our voices fill the stands.
This is no happy parting, but a battle-scarred farewell
though victory hopes are mingled with the tears
And I, like you, will stand here as the final whistle blows
with memories which echo down the years...

The Chelsea fans threw pennies. Old ones. Sharpened. I was eight.
A target in the South Stand with my dad
and he got rather battered as he held me close and tight
and confirmed my view that Chelsea fans were mad!
And there, on those old wooden seats, I learned to love the game.
The sights and sounds exploded in my head.
My dad was proud to have a son with football in his blood –
but two short years later, he was dead.

Eleven. I went on my own. (My friends liked chess and stuff.)
'Now don't go in the North Stand!' said my mum.
But soon I did. Kit Napier's corner curled into the net.
Oh God. The Bournemouth Boot Boys! Better run...
Then Villa in the big crunch game. A thirty thousand crowd.
Bald Lochhead scored, but we still won the day.
Then up, and straight back down again. Brian Powney, brave
and squat.
T.Rex, DMs and scarf on wrist, OK?

And then the world was wonderful. Punk rock and Peter Ward!
And sidekick 'Spider' Mellor, tall and lean.
The legendary Walsall game. Promotion. Riding high.
Southampton-Spurs: that stitch-up was obscene.

The final glorious victory. Division One at last!
Arsenal, first game, midst fevered expectation.
Those Highbury gods tore us to shreds; we learned the lesson well.
Steve Foster was our soul and inspiration!

Man City came, and Gerry Ryan waltzed through them to score
and mighty Man United bit the dust.
Notts Forest, and that Williams screamer nearly broke the net.
The Norwich quarter-final: win or bust!
And after Wembley, Liverpool were toppled one last time.
The final curtain on those happy days.
And then the years of gradual, inexorable decline –
sadly for some, the parting of the ways.

But we stayed true, as glory days turned into donkeys' years.
Young, Trusson, Tiltman, Farrington. Ee-aw!
A Wilkins free kick nearly brought us hope. 'Twas not to be.
The rot was deep and spreading to the core.
We found our voice and Lloyd was gone. Hooray! But worse to
come.
Though just how awful we were yet to know.
Dissent turned to rebellion and then to open war
as on the terrace weeds began to grow.

The Goldstone sold behind our backs! Enraged, we rose as one
against a stony northern businessman.
We drew a line, and said: ENOUGH! And as the nation watched
the final battle for our club began.
We fought him to a standstill. Fans United. All for one.
A nation's colours joined: a glorious sight.
And, finally, the stubborn, stony Archer moved his ground
and made way for our own collective Knight.

The battle's only just begun, but we have won the war.
Our club, though torn asunder, will survive.
And I salute each one of you who stood up and said NO!
And fought to keep the Albion alive.
And one day, when our new home's built, and we are storming back
A bunch of happy fans without a care.

We'll look back on our darkest hour and raise our glasses high
and say with satisfaction: we were there.

But first we have to face today. The hardest day of all.
Don't worry if you can't hold back the tears!
We must look to the future, in dignity and peace
as well as mourn our home of ninety years.
For me the Goldstone has an extra special memory
of the football soulmate I so briefly had.
He christened me John Charles and taught me to love the game.
This one's for Bill. A poet. And my dad.

He's a substitute

At the start of the 1965/66 season, the football league introduced a new law allowing clubs to use one substitute in matches. Peter Leggett was Albion's first ever substitute, although he was unused in the opening match of the season at Mansfield Town on Saturday 21 August. Leggett was also an unused sub for the second match of the season, at Queen's Park Rangers, before he was promoted to the starting line up for the third game of the season. In the same match, Jim Oliver became Albion's first ever used substitute. With 10 minutes left to play against Hull City at the Goldstone Ground on Saturday 28 August 1965, manager Archie Macaulay sent on utility man Oliver in place of forward Bill Cassidy, who had scored a second-half goal. Oliver's introduction didn't stop Albion from slumping to a 2-1 reverse, a defeat which saw Macaulay's side without a single point and at the foot of the Third Division.

Curious irony of 1948

Albion suffered their worst ever season in 1948/49 – they finished bottom of the Football League and were forced to seek re-election – but ironically, the club enjoyed their highest ever aggregate and average gate at the Goldstone Ground that year. Post-war rationing was still in force in the UK, but life was slowly returning to normal after the horrors of the Second World War. A total of 241,139 passed through the Goldstone turnstiles, giving the club a five-figure average for only the third time in their history (see 'First five-figure average', page 32). The average of

11,483 represented an increase of 3266 on the previous season's average gate. The increase continued the following season, when Albion were much more successful on the pitch, finishing sixth in the Fourth Division, and the average crowd at the Goldstone went up to 17,729.

Right-hander lands Alan a job

Alan Mullery's temper landed him in trouble on more than one occasion. In 1968 he became the first England player to be sent off, when he received his marching orders for retaliation in a European Championship defeat to Yugoslavia. From time to time, it also landed him in hot water with the Football Association after he called time on an illustrious playing career with Fulham and Tottenham Hotspur to become a manager. However, it was the same temper that helped Mullery land the job as Albion manager in July 1976. Chairman Mike Bamber recalled seeing the midfielder strike a team-mate while playing a match for Fulham at the Goldstone Ground in January 1973, a match that Mullery and Co won 5-1! Bamber thought Mullery's will-to-win attitude would serve him well as a manager. Mullery explained in 2005, 'I actually hit one of my Fulham team-mates when we were playing Brighton. Mike was impressed that I was so keen to win and thought it would be a good idea if I became the manager.' When Bamber phoned to offer him the job, Mullery's response was, 'I'd walk to Brighton to see you'. Bamber's instincts proved to be good, as Mullery led Albion to promotion to Division Two in 1977 and into the top flight for the first time in their history in 1979.

Albion's first loan player

In 1966, the Football League introduced new regulations to allow clubs to sign players on loan for a maximum of three months. Albion's first ever loan signing was West Ham United inside forward Brian Dear, who joined the club in March 1967 and scored an impressive five goals in seven matches. However, Albion were reluctant to pay the £20,000 fee being asked by his parent club. In 2002/03, the club made their first ever season-long loan signing, bringing in Arsenal's Irish youngster Graham Barrett.

Champions II

Albion won their first ever Football League championship in 1957/58 when they clinched the Division Three South title, and with it, promotion to Division Two for the first time in the club's history. They finished two points clear of second-placed Brentford, and in those days the second-placed club were not promoted. Only the champions of Division Three South and Division Three North were promoted to Division Two. Albion themselves had suffered from this rule in 1953/54 and 1955/56, when they'd finished Division Three South runners-up to Ipswich Town and Leyton Orient respectively. In 1957/58, needing a victory to clinch the championship, Albion did it in style, recording a 6-0 victory over Watford on Wednesday 30 April 1958. A then-record Goldstone league crowd saw Adrian Thorne smash five goals; Glen Wilson, with a penalty, scored the other.

Football League Division Three South 1957/58

Team	P	W	D	L	F	A	W	D	L	F	A	Points
Albion	**46**	**13**	**6**	**4**	**52**	**30**	**11**	**6**	**6**	**36**	**34**	**60**
Brentford	46	15	5	3	52	24	9	5	9	30	32	58
Plymouth Argyle	46	17	4	2	43	17	8	4	11	24	31	58
Swindon Town	46	14	7	2	47	16	7	8	8	32	34	57
Reading	46	14	5	4	52	23	7	8	8	27	28	55
Southampton	46	16	3	4	78	31	6	7	10	34	41	54
Southend United	46	14	5	4	56	26	7	7	9	34	32	54
Norwich City	46	11	9	3	41	28	8	6	9	34	42	53

	P	W	D	L	F	A	W	D	L	F	A	Pts
Bournemouth & BA	46	16	5	2	54	24	5	4	14	27	50	51
QPR	46	15	6	2	40	14	3	8	12	24	51	50
Newport County	46	12	6	5	40	24	5	8	10	33	43	48
Colchester United	46	13	5	5	45	27	4	8	11	32	52	47
Northampton Town	46	13	1	9	60	33	6	5	12	27	46	44
Crystal Palace	46	12	5	6	46	30	3	8	12	24	42	43
Port Vale	46	12	6	5	49	24	4	4	15	18	34	42
Watford	46	9	8	6	34	27	4	8	11	25	50	42
Shrewsbury Town	46	10	6	7	29	25	5	4	14	20	46	40
Aldershot	46	7	9	7	31	34	5	7	11	28	55	40
Coventry City	46	10	9	4	41	24	3	4	16	20	57	39
Walsall	46	10	7	6	37	24	4	2	17	24	51	37
Torquay United	46	9	7	7	33	34	2	6	15	16	40	35
Gillingham	46	12	5	6	33	24	1	4	18	19	57	35
Millwall	46	6	6	11	37	36	5	3	15	26	55	31
Exeter City	46	10	4	9	37	35	1	5	17	20	64	31

Team of nicknames

Most players' nicknames are made simply by shortening names or adding an 'a', 'o', 'y' or 'ie' to the first syllable of their forename or surname. Such names include 'Catt' (Chris Cattlin), 'Zamo' (Bobby Zamora), 'Lawro' (Mark Lawrenson), 'Willo' (Gary Williams), 'Rollo' (Andy Rollings), 'Fozzie' (Steve Foster) 'Macca' (Paul McShane, Paul McCarthy and others) and 'Watto' (Paul Watson). However, supporters or team-mates have given a little more thought to the pet names for some players.

1. Bob 'Pom Pom' Whiting
A hero in both football and military terms, Whiting earned the nickname 'Pom Pom' because of his tremendous kicking ability. Indeed, legend has it he once cleared the opposition crossbar from his own penalty area. The six-footer, regarded by Albion historians as one of the best goalkeepers to play for the club, made 320 appearances between 1908 and 1915. In 1914 he enlisted in the army to fight in the Great War and, like so many, was tragically killed in action. Aged just 34, Whiting was mortally wounded by enemy shell fire at Vimy Ridge in 1917.

2. John 'Football Genius' Crumplin
Right-winger Crumplin arrived at Albion from Bognor Regis Town in March 1987, in a rather modest transfer deal worth £6000. His early displays for the club made him the target of the supporters' frustrations and they sarcastically christened him 'Football Genius'. However, as the 1980s drew to a close, Albion boss Barry Lloyd began playing Crumplin at right back, where he excelled, and the former bricklayer made the position his own for nearly four seasons. The 'Football Genius' tag took off, and Albion fanzine *Gulls Eye* even printed t-shirts in honour of Crumplin. The pinnacle of his Albion career was undoubtedly the afternoon he shackled Liverpool and England winger John Barnes as Albion drew 2-2 with the Reds at Anfield in a fourth round FA Cup tie on 26 January 1991 (they lost the replay 3-2 aet).

3. Dan 'Tickle' Harding
Mr Tickle was the Mr Men character with very long arms, and Harding's youth team-mates picked up on this similar trait in their left-footed colleague. Shortened to 'Tickle', the name stuck as he

graduated from the youth team to the club's professional ranks. In 2005, he left Albion for Leeds United, but it's not known if his Elland Road team-mates still call him Tickle.

4. Paul 'Tank' Clark

The nickname 'Tank' couldn't have been any more apt for this armour-plated, bone-crunching, fierce-shooting, powerhouse midfielder. Stern-jawed Essex boy Clark became a firm favourite of the Goldstone crowd as he helped Albion win promotion to the First Division in 1979. He returned to his original club, Southend, in 1982, having made 93 appearances and scored nine goals for Albion. The most memorable was a superb goal against Tottenham Hotspur at the Goldstone in April 1978.

5. Danny 'Driscoll' Cullip

Most of the adjectives used to describe Paul Clark can also be used to paint a fairly accurate picture of Danny Cullip. A never-say-die defender, shaven-headed Cullip was the rock on which Albion won three promotions (2001, 2002 and 2004). A rugged stopper, Cullip would strike fear into the hearts of the hardest opposing forwards. Team-mates nicknamed Cullip and his equally fearsome midfield colleague Charlie Oatway 'The Driscoll Brothers' after the London gangster duo in the BBC comedy Only Fools and Horses.

6. Gary 'Grease' Stevens

Long hair and perms were all the fashion with the older players when Gary Stevens arrived at Albion as an apprentice in 1978, having been released by Ipswich Town. The 16-year-old new boy came sporting the shorter hairstyle of the day, influenced by the hit movie of the year, Grease, and bore a striking resemblance to the lead actor in the film, John Travolta.

7. Clive 'Flash' Walker

Clive Walker earned the nickname 'Flash' following unsubstantiated rumours of an alleged flashing incident in the 1970s. The allegation is completely unfounded but football supporters, being unforgiving souls, still referred to Walker as 'Flash' when he arrived at the Goldstone in time for the 1990/91 season. Former Chelsea legend Walker, who made 130 appearances for Albion before departing in 1993, isn't the only Flash to have played for the club. Dennis Gordon – also a stalwart on the right, but in the halcyon days of the

1950s – was also known as 'Flash', but for different reasons. The veteran of 293 games and 64 goals was named after the comic-strip character Flash Gordon.

8. Peter 'Whizz' Ward
One of the all-time favourites, if not the all-time favourite, Peter Ward had the standard 'Wardy' nickname, but in honour of his lightning speed, he was also christened 'Whizz' by his team-mates, after the comic-strip character Billy Whizz.

9. Richie 'The Bear' Barker
Richie Barker arrived at Brighton when the club were in their first season of exile at Gillingham in December 1997. Struggling at the bottom of the Third Division, they were desperate for a goal-scorer, but Barker looked anything but as he failed to score in his first 15 appearances for the club. With the hecklers on his back, Barker's days looked numbered, but two goals in the final two matches of the 1997/98 season earned him a one-year contract. Barker then hit a purple patch to score 12 goals, finish joint leading scorer and earn the nickname 'The Bear'. Having won the supporters over, Barker departed for Macclesfield Town with the blessing of the Albion faithful – he wanted to return to his native north to be closer to his sick father – and when he lined up against Albion the following season, he received a generous ovation from the club's supporters.

10. Richard 'The Duke' Carpenter
Known to the fans as 'Chippy' (or 'Chippie', as he himself likes to spell it) because of the obvious connotations of his surname, Carpenter is also known in the dressing room by his team-mates as 'The Duke', because of his love of the country and antiques. In an age of flash footballers with a love of 'bling', 'The Duke', with his encyclopaedic knowledge of antiques, is more likely to go for the real thing and is an avid collector of furniture, pugilist prints, snuff boxes and walking canes.

11. Ian 'Spider' Mellor
Ian Mellor was the perfect partner for the prolific Peter 'Whizz' Ward. Standing 6ft 1ins tall, Mellor showed a brilliant pair of feet for such a tall man, and because of this (and his long legs) the Albion supporters christened him 'Spider'. In 150 games between 1974 and 1978, 'Spider' netted 35 goals.

There are many other great Albion nicknames. Gerry Fell (1974-77) was known as (Charlie) Farley after the character in The Two Ronnies, because he was a fan of the show. Gary Hart (1998-) was christened 'Cod Eyes' or 'Iggy The Iguana' because of his big eyes. Brian Horton arrived at the Goldstone Ground from Port Vale with the nickname 'Nobby'. Gary Chivers (1988-93) was known as 'Charlie' because he was alleged to have a likeness to the famous actor Charlie Chaplin. Because of his quick turn of pace, defender Chris Ramsey (1980-84) was known as 'Yifter', after Miruts Yifter (the Shifter), the 5000- and 10,000-metre champion at the 1980 Moscow Olympics. Teddy Maybank (1977-79) was known as 'Penguin', allegedly because he walked and danced like one, but also because of his love of fish. Michael Robinson (1980-83) and Andy Ritchie (1980-83) were nicknamed 'Fred' and 'Barney' respectively, after the characters from the Flintstones, due to their size comparison and because they were always out together.

Siblings III

Durham-born brothers Joe and Glen Wilson spent close to a combined total of 70 years in the service of Brighton & Hove Albion, in a variety of roles. Both started out as players. Inside-right Joe signed from Newcastle United in May 1936 for a fee of £450 and made 353 appearances for Albion, scoring 49 goals, before hanging his boots up in 1947, when he was immediately appointed as assistant to manager Tommy Cook and trainer Alex Wilson (no relation). He became head trainer in 1952 before becoming chief scout in 1970, and eventually retired in 1974. Don Welsh signed Glen in September 1949. Glen was serving in the army at the time, and had impressed in a friendly for Farnham Town against Albion's 'A' team. He made 436 appearances, many of them as captain, scoring 28 goals. He left Albion to become player-manager at Exeter City in 1960 but after an unsuccessful time in Devon he returned to the Albion as part of the backroom staff in 1966. He remained with the club in a variety of roles, including kit man, trainer and caretaker manager, until the end of the 1985/86 season when he was given his notice by the board of that era, as part of a cost-cutting drive. Both brothers died in Brighton, Joe in 1984 and Glen in 2006.

Bat and football

Nine players have played first-class cricket as well as playing professional football for Albion. Don Bates, Tommy Cook, Denis Foreman and Ken Suttle are probably the most successful of these. Bates took 880 wickets during 21 years (1950-71) at Sussex CCC; Cook scored 20,198 runs for Sussex between 1922 and 1937; South African Foreman spent 15 years with Sussex from 1952 as a middle order batsman; and Suttle was unfortunate not to play test cricket for England. Graham Cross was the last of what appears to be a dying breed in the modern era of pro football. A case in point came in 2004, when Albion striker Joe Gatting (son of former Albion defender Steve and nephew of former England cricket captain Mike Gatting) had to choose between professional football and cricket. He opted for an apprenticeship with Albion, but still plays county league cricket in the summer months (in the same side as dad Steve) to keep fit. The full list of Albion cricketers is as follows:

Albion players' cricket records

Player	Played cricket for	Albion apps	Albion goals
Tommy Allsopp (1905-07)	Leicestershire and Norfolk	103	11
Don Bates (1950-62)	Sussex	21	1
Harry Brophy (1936-38)	Surrey	1	0
Edwin Clare (1905-06)	Nottinghamshire	28	0
Tommy Cook (1921-29)	Sussex	209	123
Graham Cross (1976-77)	Leicestershire	56	4
Denis Foreman (1952-62)	Sussex	219	69
George Leach (1904-05 & 1909)	Sussex	5	1
Ken Suttle (1949)	Sussex	3	0

Albion's all-Irish international XI

Albion have had a large number of Irish players throughout the years, with 18 players being capped for Ireland, Eire or Northern Ireland while in the employ of the Albion over the years. This 20-man squad also includes Gerry Armstrong and Frank Stapleton, Northern Ireland and Republic of Ireland legends who played for Albion after their international careers had drawn to a close.

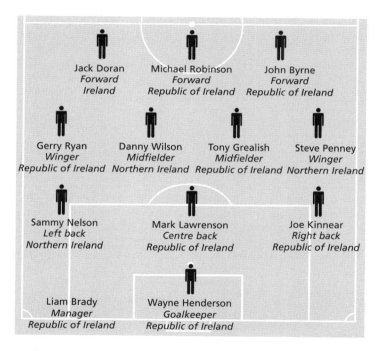

Subs: *Charlie Webb (Inside left, Ireland), Jimmy Hopkins (Inside left, Ireland), Jimmy Magill (Right back, Northern Ireland), Willie Irvine (Forward, Northern Ireland), Sammy Morgan (Forward, Northern Ireland), Kieran O'Regan (Republic of Ireland), Gary Howlett (Republic of Ireland), Frank Stapleton* (Forward, Republic of Ireland), Gerry Armstrong* (Forward, Northern Ireland)*

* Stapleton and Armstrong were not capped while on Albion's books, only prior to their arrival at the club.

Champions III

Albion picked up their second Football League championship win in season 1964/65, when they won promotion from Division Four. They clinched it on Saturday 26 April with a 3-1 win over Darlington at the Goldstone Ground. A crowd of 31,423 saw Jimmy Collins, Jack Smith and Wally Gould score in the victory; they were also three of six players to reach double figures in the scoring charts – Bill Cassidy, Johnny Goodchild and Bobby Smith were the others.

Football League Division Four Table 1964/65

Team	P	W	D	L	F	A	W	D	L	F	A	Points
Albion	**46**	**18**	**5**	**0**	**68**	**20**	**8**	**6**	**9**	**34**	**37**	**63**
Millwall	46	13	10	0	45	15	10	6	7	33	30	62
York City	46	20	1	2	63	21	8	5	10	28	35	62
Oxford United	46	18	4	1	54	13	5	11	7	33	31	61
Tranmere Rovers	46	20	2	1	72	20	7	4	12	27	36	60
Rochdale	46	15	4	4	46	22	7	10	6	28	31	58
Bradford Park Avenue	46	14	8	1	52	22	6	9	8	34	40	57
Chester City	46	19	1	3	75	26	6	5	12	44	55	56
Doncaster Rovers	46	13	6	4	46	25	7	5	11	38	47	51
Crewe Alexandra	46	11	8	4	55	34	7	5	11	35	47	49

Torquay United	46	11	5	7	41	33	10	2	11	29	37	49
Chesterfield	46	13	5	5	36	22	7	3	13	22	48	48
Notts County	46	12	7	4	43	23	3	7	13	18	50	44
Wrexham	46	12	5	6	59	37	5	4	14	25	55	43
Hartlepool United	46	11	10	2	44	28	4	3	16	17	57	43
Newport County	46	14	5	4	54	26	3	3	17	31	55	42
Darlington	46	14	2	7	52	30	4	4	15	32	57	42
Aldershot	46	14	3	6	46	25	1	4	18	18	59	37
Bradford City	46	9	2	12	37	36	3	6	14	33	52	32
Southport	46	5	9	9	35	45	3	7	13	23	44	32
Barrow	46	9	4	10	30	38	3	2	18	29	67	30
Lincoln City	46	8	4	11	35	33	3	2	18	23	66	28
Halifax Town	46	9	4	10	37	37	2	2	19	17	66	28
Stockport County	46	8	4	11	30	34	2	3	18	14	53	27

No goal

Club captain Joe Leeming played 238 games for Albion between 1908 and 1914 but amazingly, the full back did not score one solitary goal for the club, creating a club record for the most appearances by an outfield player without a goal.

Record transfer fees paid II

Albion paid out their first ever four-figure transfer fee for the services of Indian-born British national Eric Lancelotte. He had played for Albion in wartime matches in the 1941/42 season, but returned to his club of registration, Charlton Athletic, at the end of the hostilities. In February 1948, Don Welsh paid a club record fee of £3250 for the play-making inside-forward, smashing the previous record of £650 set in 1925. Lancelotte's 15 goals from 62 appearances didn't tell the full story, as he created plenty more for his team-mates. Lancelotte remained with Albion for two years, but it was only six months into that stay that his fee was topped when Welsh paid out £5000 for Newcastle United midfielder Johnny McNichol in August 1948. This turned out to be a supreme piece of business, for the classy inside-forward played 165 times for Albion, scoring 39 goals, before Chelsea paid a record fee received of £12,000 plus Jimmy Leadbetter in August 1952. The £7000 signings of Matt McNeill from Barnsley in July 1953 and Ian McNeill (no relation) from Leicester City in March 1959 bettered McNichol's fee.

Albion's Football League record

Albion's record in the Football League is listed opposite. It includes nine promotions and eight relegations. Albion's worst ever season came in 1947/48 when they finished bottom of the Fourth Division and were forced to seek re-election. Other Football League clubs voted for Albion, second-bottom Norwich City or one of the clubs seeking election to the Football League (Bath City, Bridgend Town, Chelmsford City, Colchester United, Gillingham, Lovells Athletic, Merthyr Tydfil, Peterborough United, Worcester City and Yeovil Town). In those days, the football league was virtually a closed shop and Albion received the support of their fellow members. They polled 47 votes, as did Norwich City, while just four votes went to the clubs seeking election. Albion's best finish came in the 1981/82 season, when the club finished 13th in Division One under the guidance of Mike Bailey. The Albion boss, who was criticised by some sections of Albion's support because his style of play wasn't attractive enough, even had Albion as high as 6th in the table and at one point was eyeing a UEFA Cup spot.

1921-1958	Division Three North
1958-1962	Division Two
1962-1963	Division Three
1963-1965	Division Four
1965-1972	Division Three
1972-1973	Division Two
1973-1977	Division Three
1977-1979	Division Two
1979-1983	Division One
1983-1987	Division Two
1987-1988	Division Three
1988-1992	Division Two
1992-1996	Division Two*
1996-2001	Division Three*
2001-2002	Division Two*
2002-2003	Division One*
2003-2004	Division Two*
2004-2006	Championship*⁺

* Denotes post-Premiership era.
⁺ Denotes post-2004 Football League rebranding.

Cloughie's clearout

Brian Clough was appointed manager of Brighton & Hove Albion on 1 November 1973, amid huge media interest. Clough had previously led Derby County to the Football League championship, but left the Baseball Ground after falling out with Rams chairman Sam Longston over his media commitments. His subsequent arrival at Brighton was a major coup for chairman Mike Bamber and a huge surprise to the football public. Such was the fervour in Sussex that Clough's first match in charge saw Albion's home gate leap from 6,417 to 16,017. He brought with him his assistant Peter Taylor, who quickly established that Clough and he were dealing with a squad of players who were 'a bunch of amateurs and layabouts'. They drew their initial conclusions after taking stock of the squad in an overnight stay at the White Hart Hotel in Lewes. They even asked long-serving club trainer Glen Wilson to dish the dirt on them, but, loyal to the players, Wilson kept tight-lipped, even instructing the landlord to serve him from a pre-placed bottle of cold tea instead of whiskey as Clough and Taylor looked to loosen him up with a little alcohol. Clough and Taylor ended the evening slightly sozzled, but Wilson walked tall. Nonetheless, few players survived the cull instigated by the new management duo. Peter O'Sullivan and Tony Towner were the notable survivors of the 'Cloughie Clearout'. Perhaps Clough's attitude to the Albion squad can best be ascertained from the following quote he gave not long after taking charge: 'If you threaten certain spiv players, you must carry it out and not let them get away with it. A football team only has 11 players. It just needs one bad 'un to affect the rest. In ICI, with thousands and thousands of people, you can afford to carry scoundrels. Not in a football team.' Clough's tenure at Brighton lasted just over eight months, until Leeds United lured him away to replace England-bound Don Revie. He might have gone earlier, as Iran made a bid to make him their national team coach, but that move was blocked by Albion's board. Peter Taylor remained with Albion. Reports suggested Clough virtually trebled his salary when he left, and Albion were to receive £75,000 in compensation. This was never forthcoming, and Albion eventually received £45,000 when agreement was reached in an out-of-court settlement in December 1975. Whatever, it proved to be a complete waste of money. Clough's tenure at Elland Road lasted just 44 days and he later admitted that he had made a mistake leaving Brighton. He always maintained Mike Bamber was the best chairman he ever worked with.

The Liverpools come to town

Football was suspended during the First World War, but during the Second World War the decision was taken by the authorities to continue with matches wherever possible, in order to help the nation's morale. This was fraught with problems. Air raids often caused matches to be shortened or even abandoned altogether and, with players being called up for military service, the lack of personnel often saw clubs calling on the services of other teams' players who were stationed nearby. Albion were no exception. Perhaps the best example of this was when several Liverpool players who were serving with the King's Liverpool Regiment were posted to Newhaven. The 34-team Football League Regional Competition (South) was decided on goal average. This was because there were no set fixtures and matches between the clubs were arranged on an ad hoc basis, meaning teams ended up playing a different total number of games. When the Liverpool players came to town, Albion were bottom of the table. However, with eight Liverpool players appearing in the side that season, eight wins, two draws and just one defeat helped Albion climb to a respectable 27th in the table. In a very complicated arrangement, results in the Football League Regional Competition (South) also counted towards a Football League South, which was decided by points, and eight teams entered. Albion topped this table, and won a challenge match against second-placed Watford 4-1 with help from their Merseyside friends.

Ten in a row for Bobby

In 2001/02, Bobby Zamora set a new club record when he scored goals in 10 successive appearances for the club. He began his run with a goal in the 2-2 draw at Notts County on 23 October, and then scored in the next nine matches he played, against Colchester United, Bristol City, Port Vale, Shrewsbury Town, Peterborough United, Swindon Town, Bury, Rushden & Diamonds and Chesterfield. His first blank game was the away match with Queen's Park Rangers on Boxing Day, which Albion drew 0-0. The previous record was eight matches, a record shared by four players since it was set in 1931/32 by Arthur Attwood (who beat the original record of six successive matches, set by Frank McAvoy in the club's first ever season of 1901/02). Attwood repeated the feat the following season, and was matched by Bernard Moore (1945/46), Peter Harburn (1955/56) and Cyril Thompson (1950/51).

TV tangle

Albion's Division One match at Aston Villa on 22 October 1980 had been scheduled to be one of the matches featured on a highlights programme the following day, but the plans had to be cancelled when Albion would not agree to wear shirts that didn't bear the name of their sponsors, British Caledonian. Albion fans wouldn't have been too disappointed about missing out, as the team went down 4-1 to the West Midlands club. In those days, the football authorities were strongly against sponsorship – how things change – and later in the season the Football Association fined Newcastle United and Bolton Wanderers for wearing sponsored shirts in the FA Cup.

Scandal number two

On 9 December 1905, Albion were drawn against Glossop in the FA Cup fourth qualifying round. It was the first time the club had faced Football League opposition, and a goal from Billy Yates ensured a 1-0 win for Albion. However, it was events off the pitch that day that would later grab the newspaper headlines. Albion's secretary-manager (as they were termed circa 1905) was Frank Walford-Scott. He had only been in the job for eight months when Albion travelled for the cup tie where Albion, in the form of Walford-Scott and players Mark Mellors, Bob Innes and Edwin Clare, were alleged to have made an illegal approach to sign a Glossop player named Ross. A Football Association commission found Walford-Scott, three Albion players, Ross and the referee (who had acted as a go-between in the approach) guilty of the misdemeanour. Albion were fined £10 to cover the costs of the inquiry and Walford-Scott was suspended from duties for 15 weeks (although he missed just four matches, as the suspension largely covered the close-season period 16 April to 1 August 1906). The players involved were fined £2 each, while the referee suffered the harshest punishment: Mr A Colyer was suspended for nine months.

Best League Cup performance

Albion's record in the League Cup over the years hasn't exactly been one to shout about. They lost to lower-division opposition in four successive seasons between 1988/89 and 1991/92 (Southend United, Brentford, Northampton Town and Brentford again) and as recently as 2005/06 crashed out to League Two minnows Shrewsbury Town, but in 1976/77 they enjoyed a fine run in the competition under the guidance of Alan Mullery. After disposing of Fourth Division Southend United over two legs, Third Division Albion knocked out First Division opponents Ipswich Town (after a replay) and West Bromwich Albion, in rounds two and three, before Derby County arrived in town for the fourth round. A sell-out crowd of 33,500 saw Peter Ward fire Albion ahead after just 37 seconds, beating future Albion keeper Graham

Moseley, but County (league champions two seasons previously) forced a replay and narrowly saw off Albion 2-1 at the Baseball Ground. That equalled Albion's best showing in the competition during 1966/67 season, when Albion were beaten 8-0 by Northampton in round four. They bettered it two seasons later, when they reached the fifth round of the competition via the slightly easier passage of Millwall, Burnley and Peterborough United. On Wednesday 13 December, Albion travelled to face league champions and League Cup holders Nottingham Forest at the City Ground. John McGovern put the home side ahead; Peter Ward equalised early in the second half; but Forest scored twice to win the tie 3-1. A huge following of 5,000 made the trip to Nottingham, but it should have been more. Two of three Seagulls Specials – the charter trains which took fans by rail to Albion's away matches – failed to make it to Nottingham because of a broken-down train just north of Brent. About 1000 fans missed out, and spent nearly three hours stuck on the track in north London. They eventually arrived back in Brighton at 1.30am the following morning, cold, tired and hungry. The trains had no lighting, no heating for much of the return journey, the toilets failed and there was no food available on board. A red-faced British Rail apologised to supporters in an open letter in *The Argus*, gave supporters a full refund and compensation for their tickets and set up a screening of the game at Hove Town Hall. They also ran a cut-priced Seagull Special to the league match with Charlton Athletic on 23 December. As *Argus* reporter John Vinicombe rightly pointed out, it was the Albion fans – who showed remarkable restraint under terrible conditions – who emerged with the most credit.

Highest reserve attendance

It would probably cause an outcry today, but on 11 February 1967 Albion cunningly chose a reserve team fixture with Notts County at which to put on sale tickets for a glamorous FA Cup fourth round tie with First Division Chelsea. As a result, the game attracted a record reserve crowd of 22,229, although some fans purchased their cup tickets and didn't stay to see the fixture (which, for the record, Albion won 1-0). The match with Chelsea was watched by a sell-out 35,000 crowd, who saw Albion hold their top-division opponents to a 1-1 draw. However, the replay went with the form book, and Chelsea won 4-0. Albion repeated this idea in October 1976, when they were drawn against Derby County in the League Cup. A crowd of 17,554 saw the Albion reserves beat Charlton Athletic 3-0.

Promotion 1972

Albion clinched their third Football League promotion when they finished runners-up to Aston Villa in the Third Division in 1971/72. Pat Saward's side clinched promotion in the final game of the season at home to Rochdale on Wednesday 3 May. The third highest crowd in Goldstone history witnessed John Templeman put Albion ahead in the first half. Even a second-half equaliser for the visitors didn't dampen the party atmosphere among the vast majority of the 34,766 crowd. Albion finished the season five points behind champions Aston Villa on 65 points, and equalled their best ever total, set in 1955/56. Saward's side lost just eight matches all season and finished the campaign with the best away record in the entire Football League, fully justifying the manager's pre-season policy of all-out attack.

Football League Division Three Table 1971/72

Team	P	W	D	L	F	A	W	D	L	F	A	Points
Aston Villa	46	20	1	2	45	10	12	5	6	40	22	70
Albion	**46**	**15**	**5**	**3**	**39**	**18**	**12**	**6**	**5**	**43**	**29**	**65**
Bournemouth	46	16	6	1	43	13	7	10	6	30	24	62
Notts County	46	16	3	4	42	19	9	9	5	32	25	62
Rotherham United	46	12	8	3	46	25	8	7	8	23	27	55
Bristol Rovers	46	17	2	4	54	26	4	10	9	21	30	54
Bolton Wanderers	46	11	8	4	25	13	6	8	9	26	28	50
Plymouth Argyle	46	13	6	4	43	26	7	4	12	31	38	50

	P	W	D	L	F	A	W	D	L	F	A	Pts
Walsall	46	12	8	3	38	16	3	10	10	24	41	48
Blackburn Rovers	46	14	4	5	39	22	5	13	5	15	35	47
Oldham Athletic	46	11	4	8	37	35	6	10	7	22	28	45
Shrewsbury Town	46	13	5	5	50	29	4	14	5	23	36	44
Chesterfield	46	10	5	8	25	23	8	12	3	32	34	44
Swansea City	46	10	6	7	27	21	7	12	4	19	38	44
Port Vale	46	10	10	3	27	21	3	15	5	16	38	41
Wrexham	46	10	5	8	33	26	6	14	3	26	37	40
Halifax Town	46	11	6	6	31	22	2	15	6	17	39	38
Rochdale	46	11	7	5	35	26	1	16	6	22	57	37
York City	46	8	8	7	32	22	4	15	4	25	44	36
Tranmere Rovers	46	9	7	7	34	30	1	13	9	16	41	36
Mansfield Town	46	5	12	6	19	26	3	12	8	22	37	36
Barnsley	46	6	10	7	23	30	3	12	8	9	34	36
Torquay United	46	8	6	9	31	31	2	15	6	10	38	32
Bradford City	46	6	8	9	27	32	5	16	2	18	45	32

Albion in the play-offs I

Albion have twice won through to the Football League play-offs since they were introduced in 1986/87, and on both occasions the club won through to the final (see also 'Albion in the play-offs II', page 113). In season 1990/91, Barry Lloyd's team sneaked into the end-of-season competition, thanks to a fantastic last-minute free-kick goal from Dean Wilkins in the final match of the 46-game season. Albion's final-day 2-1 win over Ipswich Town put them into a two-legged semi-final with Millwall, at the expense of Barnsley, who would have qualified but for Wilkins' heroics. (Barnsley's PA announcer sparked a pitch invasion at Oakwell when he prematurely and incorrectly announced over the tannoy that the Tykes were in the play-offs.) The first leg took place at the Goldstone Ground on Sunday 19 May. The game didn't start well for Albion, as firm favourites Millwall dominated the opening exchanges and took the lead through Paul Stephenson on 14 minutes, but Albion were on level terms once Mark Barham equalised just before half-time. Nobody would have predicted what was to happen next, as Mike Small, Clive Walker and Robert Codner netted three second-half goals in seven minutes to give Albion a 4-1 lead to take to Millwall for second leg of the semi-final. Having beaten Albion 3-0 at The Den in the league fixture between the clubs two months earlier, Millwall felt they could overturn the deficit. That belief strengthened as Millwall dominated the early stages as they had done at the Goldstone, and John McGinley put the Lions 1-0 up in the 16th minute. Albion eventually contained their hosts, however, and goals from Codner and substitute John Robinson made it 2-1 (6-2 on aggregate) to Albion, putting them through to a Wembley final against Notts County. Despite Albion's impressive displays in the semi-finals and a decent performance in the final, County proved too strong and ran out 3-1 winners, Dean Wilkins having scored a consolation for Albion in the final minute. Victory would have created a piece of history, as Albion would have become the first ever team to win promotion with a negative goal difference. Although recording more wins than defeats, most of the wins had been by a single goal, and heavy defeats at Oldham Athletic (1-6) and at home to Sheffield Wednesday (0-4) hadn't helped.

Greatest ever save?

Fans will have their own particular memories of great saves from Albion goalkeepers over the years, but two custodians – in very different circumstances – arguably saved Albion from going out of business. In 1996/97, in the relegation decider with Hereford United at Edgar Street (see 'Do or die day at Hereford', page 35), Mark Ormerod made a last-minute save to deny Adrian Foster a winning goal. The striker burst clean through on the Albion goal, but fired straight into the arms of the grateful Ormerod. Had the goal gone in, Albion would have been relegated and, with the club homeless, without any assets and haemorrhaging money, it's hard to predict whether it would have survived in the Conference – probably, but it's a moot point. Some four years earlier, it was goalkeeper Mark Beeney's transfer to Leeds United for £350,000 that saved Albion from possible extinction via a High Court winding up order. It was brought by the Inland Revenue over an unpaid tax demand of £398,000. On 20 April 1993, the day before Albion's second appearance in the High Court, Leeds boss Howard Wilkinson signed Beeney for an initial fee of £350,000, with further payments on appearances. Manager Barry Lloyd drove to the tax offices in Worthing with a banker's draft, the case was dismissed the following day and liquidation was avoided.

Cattlin fines himself

Albion manager Chris Cattlin took the unusual step of fining himself a week's wages after a disappointing goalless draw with Barnsley at the Goldstone on 20 October 1984.

Three meetings with the champions

In 1992/93, Albion, in the third tier of English football, were drawn against a Manchester United team on their way to becoming the first ever Premiership Champions in both the League Cup and the FA Cup. With the second round of the League Cup over two legs, Albion played the Red Devils three times, and all three meetings were close affairs. The first, at the Goldstone Ground on Wednesday 23 September, ended 1-1. Danny Wallace scored for the visitors in the first half, before Matthew Edwards equalised with 18 minutes remaining. Two weeks later, at Old

Trafford, United won the second leg 1-0, but United boss Alex Ferguson had some words of praise for Albion, telling *The Argus*, 'Brighton's crossing of the ball was superb. Clive Walker was a great example to younger players and Steve Foster's head kept attracting the ball like a magnet.' Albion were back at Old Trafford on 23 January 1993 for a fourth round FA Cup tie, after victory over First Division Portsmouth at the Goldstone in the previous round. Albion again went down 1-0, to a Ryan Giggs free kick, but the team did the club proud and three bumper gates meant a healthy pay day at a time when cash was in short supply at the Goldstone.

Fans United

On 8 February 1997, Albion fans organised a Fans United Day to coincide with the match against Hartlepool United at the Goldstone Ground. Fans from other clubs were encouraged to come to the Goldstone Ground to protest against the way the club was being run and in particular the sale of the Goldstone. An official crowd of 8412 flocked to the Goldstone from all four corners of the UK, with each of the 92 professional Premiership and Football League clubs represented and many more from Europe and the rest of the world. The event was a huge success, gaining a lot of positive media exposure, and on the pitch Albion recorded their biggest win of the season. The 5-0 win saw Craig Maskell score a hat trick, dedicated to the fans, with Ian Baird and Gary Hobson also on the score-sheet. Subsequent events were held at Albion's home match with Doncaster the following season, Chester a season later and at Wrexham in 2004, to highlight similar problems at those clubs.

Most points

Albion racked a record 65 points (under the old two points for a win system) in 1955/56 and again during the promotion season of 1971/72. Under the three points for a win system, the team would have recorded 94 points in 1955/56 (and they didn't even finish top) and 92 in 1971/72. The club record under the three points for a win system introduced in season 1981/82 is 92 points, collected in the Third Division championship-winning campaign in 2000/01. A season later, they were two short of this total when they managed 90 points, but they were one division higher.

Dreadful start

After winning promotion from Division Three in 1987/88, Garry Nelson gave Albion a dream start to life back in Division Two with an early goal against Bradford City in the opening game of the season at the Goldstone. However, City proved too strong, as did Albion's next seven opponents, and at eight straight defeats, this is the club's worst ever start to a season. The first win came on Saturday 1 October. Leeds United were the visitors to the Goldstone, and at half-time, a ninth straight reverse looked on the cards as United led 1-0. However, second-half goals from Garry Nelson and Kevin Bremner gave Albion a 2-1 win. From there they found their feet and Barry Lloyd's team eventually finished 19th and nine points clear of the drop zone.

Goldstone improvement

Throughout their 95-year occupancy, Albion made a number of improvements to the facilities on offer at the Goldstone Ground. A wooden West Stand was built in 1901, and three years later another wooden structure was built behind the south goal. Both remained in place until the 1950s, although the South Stand was rebuilt and raised in the 1940s. Work was completed to erect a roof on the North Stand in January 1931, and a new South Stand with 1000 seats behind terracing was built in 1954. Before the start of the 1958/59 season, with Albion entering Division Two, a new 1400-seat West Stand replaced the dated wooden structure at a cost of £32,330. It was the first phase of a three-part stand, but as it turned out only two phases (the middle and southern parts of the new grandstand) were completed, with the second phase finished in 1959. That gave the West Stand a slightly lopsided look. In 1972, new offices and dressing rooms were built into the back of the stand. When Albion reached the First Division in 1979, a 980-seat stand, nicknamed the Lego Stand, was opened in the position left vacant by the uncompleted final third of the West Stand. The temporary structure remained in place until 1985. The South Stand caught fire the evening after Albion's penultimate game of the 1979/80 season. The roof remained intact, but everything else was destroyed. It reopened on 20 December 1980 as an all-seater stand. The last major work at the Goldstone before the bulldozers moved in was in 1984, when the North Stand got a new roof at the cost of £200,000.

The halcyon days

Albion's halcyon days came in the late 1970s, when the club won promotion from Division Three to Division One inside two seasons, under the guidance of the man many consider to be the finest Albion manager of all time, Alan Mullery. Micky Adams and Billy Lane are other contenders, but Mullery achieved what no other Albion boss has ever managed by guiding the club into the top division. Promotion was won in 1976/77 with a 3-2 win over Sheffield Wednesday on Saturday 3 May in front of a crowd of 30,756. The following season, Mullery's men missed out on a second successive promotion on the final day of the season (see 'Spurs 0 Southampton 0', page 34), but Albion finally reached the heady heights of the top flight with promotion in 1978/79 (see 'Newcastle clincher', page 51).

Football League Division Three Table 1976/77

Team	P	W	D	L	F	A	W	D	L	F	A	Points	GD
Mansfield Town	46	17	6	0	52	13	11	2	10	26	29	64	+36
Albion	**46**	**19**	**3**	**1**	**63**	**14**	**6**	**8**	**9**	**20**	**26**	**61**	**+43**
Crystal Palace	46	17	5	1	46	15	6	8	9	22	25	59	+28
Rotherham United	46	11	9	3	30	15	11	6	6	39	29	59	+25
Wrexham	46	15	6	2	47	22	9	4	10	33	32	58	+26
Preston North End	46	15	4	4	48	21	6	8	9	16	22	54	+21
Bury	46	15	2	6	41	21	8	6	9	23	38	54	+5
Sheffield Wednesday	46	15	4	4	39	18	7	5	11	26	37	53	+10

Lincoln City	46	12	9	2	50	30	7	5	11	27	40	52	+7
Shrewsbury Town	46	13	7	3	40	21	5	4	14	25	38	47	+6
Swindon Town	46	12	6	5	48	33	3	9	11	20	42	45	-7
Gillingham	46	11	8	4	31	21	5	4	14	24	43	44	-9
Chester City	46	14	3	6	28	20	4	5	14	20	38	44	-10
Tranmere Rovers	46	10	7	6	31	23	3	10	10	20	30	43	-2
Walsall	46	8	7	8	39	32	5	8	10	18	33	41	-8
Peterborough United	46	11	4	8	33	28	2	11	10	22	37	41	-10
Oxford United	46	9	8	6	34	29	3	7	13	21	36	39	-10
Chesterfield	46	10	6	7	30	20	4	4	15	26	44	38	-8
Port Vale	46	9	7	7	29	28	2	9	12	18	43	38	-24
Portsmouth	46	8	9	6	28	26	3	5	15	25	44	36	-17
Reading	46	10	5	8	29	24	3	4	16	20	49	35	-24
Northampton Town	46	9	4	10	33	29	4	4	15	27	46	34	-15
Grimsby Town	46	10	6	7	29	22	2	3	18	16	47	33	-24
York City	46	7	8	8	25	34	3	4	16	25	55	32	-39

continued

Football League Division Two Table 1977/78

Team	P	W	D	L	F	A	W	D	L	F	A	Points	G D
Bolton Wanderers	42	16	4	1	39	14	8	6	7	24	19	58	+30
Southampton	42	15	4	2	44	16	7	9	5	26	23	57	+31
Tottenham Hotspur	42	13	7	1	50	19	7	9	5	33	30	56	+34
Albion	**42**	**15**	**5**	**1**	**43**	**21**	**7**	**7**	**7**	**20**	**17**	**56**	**+25**
Blackburn Rovers	42	12	4	5	33	16	4	9	8	23	44	45	-4
Sunderland	42	11	6	4	36	17	3	10	8	31	42	44	+8
Stoke City	42	13	5	3	38	16	3	5	13	15	33	42	+4
Oldham Athletic	42	9	10	2	32	20	4	6	11	22	38	42	-4
Crystal Palace	42	9	7	5	31	20	4	8	9	19	27	41	+3
Fulham	42	9	8	4	32	19	5	5	11	17	30	41	0
Burnley	42	11	6	4	35	20	4	4	13	21	44	40	-8
Sheffield United	42	13	4	4	38	22	3	4	14	24	51	40	-11
Luton Town	42	11	4	6	35	20	3	6	12	19	32	38	+2
Leyton Orient	42	8	11	2	30	20	2	7	12	13	29	38	-6
Notts County	42	10	9	2	36	22	1	7	13	18	40	38	-8
Millwall	42	8	8	5	23	20	4	6	11	26	37	38	-8
Charlton Athletic	42	11	6	4	38	27	2	6	13	17	41	38	-13
Bristol Rovers	42	10	7	4	40	26	3	5	13	21	51	38	-16
Cardiff City	42	12	6	3	32	23	1	6	14	19	48	38	-20

Blackpool	*42*	*7*	*8*	*6*	*35*	*25*	*5*	*5*	*11*	*24*	*35*	*37*	*-1*
Mansfield Town	*42*	*6*	*6*	*9*	*30*	*34*	*4*	*5*	*12*	*19*	*35*	*31*	*-20*
Hull City	*42*	*6*	*6*	*9*	*23*	*25*	*2*	*6*	*13*	*11*	*27*	*28*	*-18*

continued

Football League Division Two Table 1978/79

Team	P	W	D	L	F	A	W	D	L	F	A	Points	GD
Crystal Palace	42	12	7	2	30	11	7	12	2	21	13	57	+27
Albion	42	16	3	2	44	11	7	7	7	28	28	56	+33
Stoke City	42	11	7	3	35	15	9	9	3	23	16	56	+27
Sunderland	42	13	3	5	39	19	9	8	4	31	25	55	+26
West Ham United	42	12	7	2	46	15	6	7	8	24	24	50	+31
Notts County	42	8	10	3	23	15	6	6	9	25	45	44	-12
Preston North End	42	7	11	3	36	23	5	7	9	23	34	42	+2
Newcastle United	42	13	3	5	34	24	4	5	12	16	31	42	-4
Cardiff City	42	12	5	4	34	23	4	5	12	22	47	42	-14
Fulham	42	10	7	4	35	19	3	8	10	15	28	41	+3
Leyton Orient	42	11	5	5	32	18	4	5	12	19	33	40	0
Cambridge United	42	7	10	4	22	15	5	6	10	22	37	40	-8
Burnley	42	11	6	4	31	22	3	6	12	20	40	40	-11
Oldham Athletic	42	10	7	4	36	23	3	6	12	16	38	39	-9
Wrexham	42	10	6	5	31	16	2	8	11	14	26	38	+3
Bristol Rovers	42	10	6	5	34	23	4	4	13	14	37	38	-12
Leicester City	42	7	8	6	28	23	3	9	9	15	29	37	-9
Luton Town	42	11	5	5	46	24	2	5	14	14	33	36	+3
Charlton Athletic	42	6	8	7	28	28	5	5	11	32	41	35	-9

Sheffield United	42	9	6	6	34	24	2	6	13	18	45	34	-17
Millwall	42	7	4	10	22	29	4	6	11	20	32	32	-19
Blackburn Rovers	42	5	8	8	24	29	5	2	14	17	43	30	-31

5000th league goal

Colin Kazim-Richards scored the Albion's 5000th league goal. The Hackney-born striker opened the scoring in a 2-1 defeat at Crewe on 25 February 2006.

Albion in the Sussex Senior Cup

Albion's reserves have won the Sussex Senior Cup on six separate occasions. The competition has been in existence since 1882/83, but Albion didn't enter until 1945/46 and didn't become regular entrants until the late 1970s. The club first won the trophy in 1988 when Albion recorded a 3-0 win over Lewes at the Goldstone Ground, which was used for the final. A goal from Dave Savage in 1992 enabled Albion to repeat the feat against Langney Sports (now Eastbourne Borough). Albion beat Peacehaven 1-0 in 1995, and Bognor Regis Town 2-0 the following year, in their last ever final at the Goldstone. After the Goldstone Ground was demolished, Eastbourne Borough hosted the Sussex Football Association's Premier Cup Final, and Albion were there in 2000 to draw 1-1 with Hastings Town after extra time. They won the trophy in a penalty shoot-out, but angry first-team boss Micky Adams awarded Hastings a moral victory. He was furious with Albion's performance and handed the champagne his team had been awarded to the non-league runners-up. Albion were back at Eastbourne Borough, lifting the trophy for the sixth time after a 2-0 victory over Worthing in 2004.

French connection II

In 2004/05, Albion began a cross-cultural tie up with French club Le Havre. Backed by the European authorities and British Government to promote Anglo-French relationships, the project included several cross-channel trips for both clubs' first teams and youth teams, and delegations from Albion's successful Football in the Community project. In 2005, Albion's first team visited Le Havre for a week's pre-season training and a friendly, played at Gonfreville L'Orcher Stadium. Albion produced a groundbreaking bilingual 20-page programme for the match, which included an introduction to Le Havre (in English) and Albion (in French) as well as messages from Albion chairman Dick Knight and Le Havre Managing Director Alain Belsoeur. Le Havre won the match 2-0, but that didn't stop Albion making another trip in the build-up to the 2005/06 season. The second match between the club's first teams was played at Le Havre, with a match between the two respective youth teams playing at Gonfreville L'Orcher Stadium. The final score between the senior sides was again 2-0 to Le Havre, but Albion's youngsters fared better: they won 2-1.

The FA Cup run of 1983

In 1983, Albion recorded their best performance in the FA Cup when they reached the final of the competition. The epic run began with a home tie in round three against Second Division Newcastle United on Saturday 8 January. Andy Ritchie opened the scoring for Albion in the second half, but Terry McDermott's equaliser meant a replay at St James's Park on the following Wednesday evening. Newcastle were expected to make home advantage pay, but a goal from Peter Ward – back at the club, on loan from Nottingham Forest – put Albion through to a fourth round meeting with Manchester City at the Goldstone Ground. An emphatic 4-0 win, thanks to goals from Jimmy Case and Neil Smillie and two from Michael Robinson, set up a fifth round tie at Anfield against Liverpool. The Reds – who hadn't lost a home cup tie since 1964 – were odds-on favourites to win the tie, underlined by their price of 9/1 to win the FA Cup. However, Albion, managed by former Liverpool player Jimmy Melia, and with one-time Anfield favourite Jimmy Case in midfield, pulled off one of the major shocks of that season's competition, beating Liverpool 2-1 in the Sunday fixture. (Everton had been also been drawn at home to Tottenham Hotspur and had played at Goodison Park on the Saturday.) Gerry Ryan opened the scoring after 32 minutes and Aussie midfielder Craig Johnston levelled the tie 20 minutes from time, before Case hit a stunning 25-yard drive past Bruce Grobbelaar to put Albion 2-1 up. They still suffered two scares in the final 20 minutes or so: Phil Neal missed a penalty and former Albion man Mark Lawrenson had a header cleared off the line by Chris Ramsey. A home quarter-final tie with Norwich City was next, and Albion won through 1-0, thanks to another goal from Case after 66 minutes. With the linesman flagging as Case ran through, the 28,800 crowd held their breath, but the goal stood – the flag had been raised for a foul on Case and referee Alan Robinson had played an advantage. For the semi-final, Melia wanted to avoid big guns Arsenal and Manchester United. He got his wish, as they were drawn together and Albion were paired with

Second Division Sheffield Wednesday. The match was played at Arsenal's Highbury Stadium on 16 April 1983 and on an unforgettable day for Albion followers in the 54,627 crowd, Melia's side triumphed 2-1, thanks to goals from Case – another rocket – and Robinson, either side of half-time and sandwiching Ante Mirocevic's 57th minute equaliser. That took Albion to Wembley and into the final (see 'FA Cup Final', page 103).

The FA Cup run of 1983

Round	Opponents	Score	Scorer(s)
Third round	Newcastle United (h)	1-1	Andy Ritchie
Third round replay	Newcastle United (a)	1-0	Peter Ward
Fourth round	Manchester City (h)	4-0	Jimmy Case, Neil Smillie, Michael Robinson
Fifth round	Liverpool (a)	2-1	Gerry Ryan
Quarter-final	Norwich City (h)	1-0	Jimmy Case
Semi-final	Sheffield Wednesday	2-1	Jimmy Case, Michael Robinson

Fozzie at the High Court

Two weeks after Albion won through to the 1983 FA Cup Final with a victory over Sheffield Wednesday in the Highbury semi-final, disaster struck for headband-wearing skipper Steve Foster when he was booked for dissent in the Division One match at Notts County on 30 April. Under the totting up procedure, Foster would be suspended for the Cup Final. Albion appealed to the Football Association, and when that was unsuccessful they went to the High Court to get the suspension rescinded. Five days before the final, Justice Vinelott ruled in favour of the FA: the ban stood. Midfielder Tony Grealish took over the captaincy for the final, leading Albion out wearing a headband in sympathy for his suspended colleague. Foster sat alongside manager Jimmy Melia on the Albion bench and saw his team-mates earn a remarkable 2-2 draw, which meant Foster finally got to play in the FA Cup Final. Free from suspension, he played in the FA Cup Final replay four days later.

FA Cup Final

Albion made their first ever Wembley appearance when they won through to the 1983 FA Cup Final (see 'The FA Cup run of 1983', page 101). After beating Sheffield Wednesday in the semi-final, Jimmy Melia's Seagulls faced Manchester United on 21 May 1983, kick-off 3pm. Albion were sponsored by British Caledonian at the time and the airline arranged for the team to travel from Brighton to Wembley by helicopter. The chopper landed at a nearby school, where a waiting bus transferred the team to the stadium. Thousands of Albion supporters made the same trip by rail or road and saw their team led out by stand-in skipper Tony Grealish, who sported a headband in sympathy for suspended captain Steve Foster (see 'Fozzie at the High Court', page 102). The game started well for Albion as Gordon Smith headed the Seagulls in front after just 14 minutes. Goals from Frank Stapleton and Ray Wilkins put United 2-1 ahead, but a dramatic 85th-minute equaliser from Gary Stevens sent the game to extra time. There was little between the two teams, and the match appeared to be heading for a replay when suddenly, Michael Robinson burst clear on goal. The Albion forward squared for his strike partner Gordon Smith. As he did so, BBC Radio 2 commentator Peter Jones uttered the words, 'And Smith must score!', words that have haunted the Scotsman ever since, as he hit his shot straight at the legs of United keeper Gary Bailey. Five days later, United won the replay 4-0.

A couple of balls

Gary Hart was signed from Stansted in 1998 for the rather modest fee of £1000, plus a new set of playing kit for his old team. That certainly proved money well spent, with Hart racking up 342 appearances and 44 goals (and counting) by the end of the 2005/06 season. That works out a rather good-value price of £2.92 per game – not counting the cost of the kit. When Paul McCarthy joined Albion as a trainee from Irish club Rockmount in July 1988, the fee was a couple of match balls. Another great piece of business, as McCarthy went on to appear 217 times for Albion and score eight goals.

Admission prices

The cheapest ticket to watch Albion's home matches has risen from 6d in 1901 to £21.50 at the start of the 2006/07 season. The price remained 6d for Albion's first 15 years of existence before rising to one shilling, which was the only rise in the first 48 years of the club's history. The switch to decimalisation in 1971 meant the cheapest entrance fee switched from six shillings to 30 pence. Albion's promotion to Division Two in 1977 saw a rise from 65 pence to £1, and this had reached £1.50 (with seats costing between £2.50 and £4.50) by the time Albion played their first match in Division One in 1979. This made the Goldstone one of the most expensive grounds in the country. In the final season at the Goldstone, the cheapest entrance ticket was £8 for a place on the terrace.

Division One debut

Albion were matched against Arsenal for their debut in the First Division on Saturday 18 August 1979, and Albion produced a special 32-page souvenir programme to commemorate the occasion. The issue cost 50 pence (instead of the regular price of 20 pence). The cover bore a shot of the Albion team, including new signings Steve Foster and John Gregory, and inside, Alan Mullery wrote about Albion joining the best league in the world.

Goalkeeping no-show

On Saturday 10 September 1988, Albion goalkeeper Perry Digweed missed a first-team game, not because he was injured or suspended, but because, as he claimed, nobody actually called him to tell him he was playing. Digweed had not featured for the first team at that point in the season, but had been recalled to the first team in place of John Keeley, who had failed a Saturday morning fitness test for on the morning of the Second Division match with Bournemouth at the Goldstone Ground. Downhearted Keeley left his team-mates to get ready for action and went to drown his sorrows at the Stadium Tavern on Old Shoreham Road. The Albion keeper had already enjoyed a meat pie and was midway through his third pint of lager, when club physiotherapist Malcolm Stuart telephoned the pub to tell Keeley he was required to play after all, due to Digweed's failure to show for the game. Albion lost the game 2-1, but Keeley wasn't culpable. He later admitted he felt absolutely fine – despite his unusual pre-match ritual.

Record transfer fees paid III

Bill Curry became Albion's first five-figure signing when he joined from Newcastle United in July 1959. The centre forward proved a worthwhile acquisition, as he scored 29 goals in 54 appearances before moving to Derby County, with Albion recouping £12,000 of their outlay. A fee of £15,000 was paid to Chelsea for centre forward Tony Nicholas in November 1960, a record that stood until August 1967 when Archie Macaulay paid £25,000 to Bolton Wanderers for central defender John Napier. Again, that was money extremely well spent, as Napier gave five years' good service and clocked up 247 senior matches. Between March 1972 and November 1974, six players arrived for record fees:

Date	Player	Bought from	Fee
March 1972	Ken Beamish	Tranmere Rovers	£25,000 plus Alan Duffy
August 1972	Barry Bridges	Millwall	£29,000
December 1973	Ronnie Welch	Burnley	£35,000*
December 1973	Harry Wilson	Burnley	£35,000*
April 1974	Ian Mellor	Norwich City	£40,000
November 1974	Ken Tiler	Chesterfield	£45,000⁺

* The deal that brought midfielder Ronnie Welch and left-back Harry Wilson to the club was a combined fee of £70,000.

⁺ Ken Tiler was swapped for Ronnie Welch and Billy McEwan, but the transfer was rated at £45,000.

First scoring sub

Substitutes were first introduced in 1965/66 season (see 'He's a substitute', page 70), but it wasn't until the following season that a player came off the bench to net a goal for Albion. Charlie Livesey was the man to do it, coming on to net the third goal in a 3-1 FA Cup third round replay win over Aldershot at the

Goldstone on 1 February 1967. The first player to score in a league match was Paul Flood the following season, when he scored the fourth and final goal in a 4-0 win over Colchester at the Goldstone Ground in a Division Three fixture on 23 August 1967.

Penalty practice

When Albion beat Swindon Town in a penalty shoot out to reach the 2004 play-off final, much of their success could be put down to a practice regime put in place by manager Mark McGhee ahead of the second leg at Withdean. Every player in the squad was made to practise spot kicks regularly in the build-up to the game until he found a routine he was comfortable with, then stick to it, memorise its intricacies (how he would walk up to the penalty spot, how he would place the ball, the number of steps backwards he would take, how he would strike the ball, which direction he would hit it) and keep practising it. McGhee felt this technique would take the pressure out of the situation for his players and remove any doubt or indecision from their minds if and when they walked up to take their kicks. He was right: Albion scored all four of their kicks in the shoot out to win 4-3 and progress to the Millennium Stadium for the final.

Celebrity fans

The Albion has a number of celebrity supporters, including TV presenters Des Lynam and Jamie Theakston, superstar DJ Norman Cook (aka Fatboy Slim), comedian Norman Wisdom, commentator Peter Brackley, actors Ralph Brown (Star Wars I, Buster, Alien 3), Chris Ellison (The Bill), Steve North (London's Burning, Eastenders), Amanda Redman (Sexy Beast and New Tricks), Mark Williams (The Fast Show and Harry Potter films) and Channel 4 newsreader Jon Snow. The two Normans – Cook and Wisdom – have also been involved with the club, as shareholder and director respectively, and Norman Cook is still a shareholder today.

Record transfer fee received III

Johnny McNichol was the first Albion player to be transferred from the club for a five-figure fee; he went to Chelsea for £12,000 plus Jimmy Leadbetter in August 1952. Eric Steele was the club's first six-figure sale, at £100,000 to Watford in 1979. Bobby Zamora became the first £1m-plus sale when he joined Tottenham Hotspur in 2003.

Date	Player	Sold to	Fee
August 1952	Johnny McNichol	Chelsea	£12,000
			plus Jimmy Leadbetter
October 1952	Jack Mansell	Cardiff City	£15,000
December 1974	Steve Govier	Grimsby Town	£16,000
May 1974	Ken Beamish	Blackburn Rovers	£26,000
February 1978	Ian Mellor	Chester City	£30,000
August 1978	Eric Potts	Preston North End	£37,000
October 1978	Tony Towner	Millwall	£65,000
October 1979	Eric Steele	Watford	£100,000
December 1979	Teddy Maybank	Fulham	£150,000
July 1980	Ray Clarke	Newcastle United	£175,000
October 1980	Peter Ward	Nottingham Forest	£450,000
August 1981	Mark Lawrenson	Liverpool	£900,000
July 2003	Bobby Zamora	Tottenham Hotspur	£1.5m
July 2005	Adam Virgo	Celtic	£1.5m

Flu epidemic causes cancellation

In the build-up to Albion's Second Division match at Stoke City on 16 September 1978, 15 of the first-team squad were struck down by a flu epidemic. The match was postponed and rescheduled for 27 September. When it was eventually played, Albion drew 2-2 with goals from Peter Ward and Teddy Maybank.

Good run, bad run

Albion went 17 matches without a defeat in the 1987/88 season. The run began on 3 October 1987 with a 2-1 win over Bury in the Third Division, and ended 18 games later on 28 December when Bristol City beat Albion 5-2 at Ashton Gate. Albion's longest run without a win was 16 games in the 1972/73 relegation season. After three draws in October, Albion suffered 13 consecutive defeats, which saw them slide from 16th position in the table to bottom, where they stayed all season. The run ended on 10 February 1973, with a 2-0 win over Luton Town.

Promotion 1988

Having finished rock bottom of the Second Division by quite a distance in 1986/87, Albion were not expected to be among the front-runners in the Third Division in 1987/88. During the close season, manager Barry Lloyd was forced to offload several of the club's better players – Terry Connor, Danny Wilson and Eric Young – but he did bring in several new faces – Kevin Bremner, Keith Dublin, Garry Nelson, Doug Rougvie, Mike Trusson and Dean Wilkins. By mid-October, there was little to suggest that Albion could bounce back at the first attempt. On Saturday 17 October, the Seagulls were 10th in the table after a dismal goalless draw with Preston North End at the Goldstone Ground. Perhaps the best supporters could hope for was a play-off place. But suddenly, Lloyd's new-look side clicked into gear. They lost just four more matches all season, and an incredible run in the final eight matches saw them drop just two points. That happened in the penultimate match of the season at Chester City, where Albion (in third place going into the game) threw away a two-goal lead. However, as the team made their way back to the dressing room they were delighted to learn that both their main rivals for the all-important second spot – Walsall and Notts County – had lost! That left Albion needing three points from their final match of the season at the first attempt. On Saturday 7 May, a crowd of 19,800 packed the Goldstone Ground and saw Albion seal their promotion back to Division Two at the first attempt. On Saturday 7 May, a crowd of 19,800 packed the Goldstone Ground and saw Albion seal their promotion with goals from Kevin Bremner and Garry Nelson in a 2-1 victory.

Football League Division Three Table 1987/88

Team	P	W	D	L	F	A	W	D	L	F	A	Points	GD
Sunderland	46	14	7	2	51	22	13	5	5	41	26	93	+44
Albion	46	15	7	1	37	16	8	8	7	32	31	84	+22

Walsall	46	15	6	2	39	22	8	7	8	29	28	82	+18
Notts County	46	14	4	5	53	24	9	8	6	29	25	81	+33
Bristol City	46	14	6	3	51	30	7	6	10	26	32	75	+15
Northampton Town	46	12	8	3	36	18	6	11	6	34	33	73	+19
Wigan Athletic	46	11	8	4	36	23	9	4	10	34	38	72	+9
Bristol Rovers	46	14	5	4	43	19	4	7	12	25	37	66	+12
Fulham	46	10	5	8	36	24	9	4	10	33	36	66	+9
Blackpool	46	13	4	6	45	27	4	10	9	26	35	65	+9
Port Vale	46	12	8	3	36	19	6	3	14	22	37	65	+2
Brentford	46	9	8	6	27	23	7	6	10	26	36	62	-6
Gillingham	46	8	9	6	45	21	6	8	9	32	40	59	+16
Bury	46	9	7	7	33	26	6	7	10	25	31	59	+1
Chester City	46	9	8	6	29	30	5	8	10	22	32	58	-11
Preston North End	46	10	6	7	30	23	5	7	11	18	36	58	-11
Southend United	46	10	6	7	42	33	4	7	12	23	50	55	-18
Chesterfield	46	10	5	8	25	28	5	5	13	16	42	55	-29
Mansfield Town	46	10	6	7	25	21	4	6	13	23	38	54	-11
Aldershot	46	12	3	8	45	32	3	5	15	19	42	53	-10
Rotherham United	46	8	8	7	28	25	4	8	11	22	41	52	-16
Grimsby Town	46	6	6	10	25	29	6	7	10	23	29	50	-10
York City	46	4	7	12	27	45	4	2	17	21	46	33	-43
Doncaster Rovers	46	6	5	12	25	36	2	4	17	15	48	33	-44

Super Sub Eric Potts

Signed from Sheffield Wednesday for £14,000 in July 1977, Eric Potts gained the nickname 'Super Sub' after he came off the subs' bench during a match with Sunderland at the Goldstone on 25 February 1978, and transformed the game with two goals inside the last half hour. Of his 41 appearances for Albion, 15 were as a substitute. Three of his seven Albion goals came in matches he began on the bench – in addition to his brace against Sunderland, he hit one in a 3-1 win over Tottenham Hotspur on 15 April 1978. In August 1978 he joined Preston North End for £37,000 – not a bad piece of business by then-manager Alan Mullery.

People's Player II

Following in the footsteps of Bert Murray (see 'People's Player I', page 29), Rod Thomas became the club's second 'People's Player' when he was signed from Carlisle United by Brian Horton in October 1998. The £25,000 transfer fee was paid from a supporter-initiated Buy a Player appeal.

He shot, he scored

There have been countless songs sung by Albion supporters during matches. 'Seagulls! Seagulls!' and the 'Albion chant' are the most popular, but one of the favourite player-related chants is the ode to record-setting striker Peter Ward. An original Albion anthem (as opposed to another club's song changed to fit the Albion), it has since been used by several other clubs up and down the country:

> *He shot*
> *He scored*
> *It must be Peter Ward*
> *Peter Ward, Peter Ward* (continue at pleasure)

Wardy's popularity across the land (the striker finished second in a 1977 nationwide popularity poll) seems to have helped the song to travel, but there are those who believe the song was originally sung in the 1970s about another Albion legend:

He's here
He's there
He's every-bloody-where
Norman Gall, Norman Gall

Another famous ode to Wardy is the following offering (sometimes the second verse is sung on its own):

Mine eyes have seen the glory of the coming of the Lord
He plays for Brighton & Hove Albion and his name is Peter Ward
Defenders tell in fear of the goals that he has scored
And the stripes go marching on, on, on!

Glory, glory, Brighton & Hove Albion
Glory, glory, Brighton & Hove Albion
Glory, glory, Brighton & Hove Albion
And the stripes go marching on, on, on!

Family affair

Five Albion players have seen their sons go on to play for the club. Sammy Booth, son of Billy, who played for the club 369 times between 1908 and 1920, was the first. He made 29 appearances in two spells between 1938 and 1949, punctuated by the Second World War. Les Jones turned out for Albion in wartime football; he was the son of Bill 'Bullet' Jones who was a team-mate of Billy Booth's and scored 69 goals in 179 appearances for Albion. More recently, Gerry Ryan, Larry May and Steve Gatting's sons – Darragh, Chris and Joe – have all played for Albion's first team.

Other rivals

Albion's main and fiercest rivals are Crystal Palace, but in recent years rivalries have developed with other clubs, usually between supporters. Portsmouth, the closest league team after Palace, were considered rivals for much of the 1980s and 1990s. The drop to the Third Division in the mid-1990s proved the catalyst for rivalry with Leyton Orient. With Albion fighting for their lives at the bottom of the Football League, a volatile 4-4 draw in March 1997 at the Goldstone Ground proved the spark. The following season, Albion failed to beat the East London club in seven league and cup meetings, which took Orient's unbeaten record against Albion to nine matches. The record ended on 14 August when Andy Crosby and Paul Rogers scored in a 2-1 win at Brisbane Road. In 2000/01 Albion had a minor rivalry with Cardiff – the two teams were both chasing promotion from Division Three. The Welsh team also poached Albion assistant manager Alan Cork, and tried to lure away striker Bobby Zamora with a string of £1m-plus bids, but Albion had the last laugh as Third Division Champions. A year later, in similar circumstances, Reading became rivals, scrapping it out at the top with Albion and trying to lure away on-loan Leicester City midfielder Junior Lewis. Once again, Albion saw off their moneybags rivals and were crowned champions. However, the following season Reading did poach midfielder Steve Sidwell and in 2003/04 took manager Steve Coppell.

Who's the greatest: Billy Lane, Alan Mullery or Micky Adams?

It's often debated as to who is Albion's greatest ever manager. Three men who are most likely to feature in any such argument are Billy Lane, Alan Mullery and Micky Adams. Their individual records are as follows:

Manager	Era	P	W	D	L	%
Billy Lane	1951-61	493	220	119	154	52.67
Alan Mullery	1976-81	249	109	66	74	52.61
Alan Mullery II	1986-87	27	7	8	12	35.8
Alan Mullery Overall	–	276	116	74	86	50.96
Micky Adams	1999-2001	125	57	34	34	54.67

The percentage is worked out on the three points for a win system, and the stats do little to solve the argument. Mullery's record from his first spell in charge is almost identical to that of Lane's. Adams's record is the best, but over the shortest period.

Bring Home the Albion

In 1997, quite soon after Dick Knight finally managed to wrestle control from Bill Archer, Albion supporters launched the Bring Home the Albion campaign. The brainchild of supporter Adrian

Newnham, it aimed to gain public support for the club's proposed move back to Brighton from their ground-sharing exile in Gillingham. Sussex residents, local businesses and local paper *The Argus* got behind the campaign. It proved a huge success as local councillors voted in favour of allowing Albion to use the city's athletics stadium at Withdean as a temporary home, so ending their exile at Gillingham. The stalwarts of the Bring Home the Albion campaign became mainstays of the supporter-driven campaigns, YES YES and Falmer For All (see 'Yes! Yes!', page 114).

Fenced in

Following trouble at the match with Tottenham Hotspur in April 1978, the club was advised by the Football Association to install fencing at the Goldstone Ground. Despite protests from supporters, metal perimeter fencing, made by Littlehampton Welding, was installed during the 1978/79 season at a cost of £30,000.

Albion in the play-offs II

In 2003/04, Albion won promotion via the play-offs. Mark McGhee's side finished fourth in the Second Division, which set up a two-legged encounter with fifth-placed Swindon Town. The first leg at the County Ground finished 1-0 to Albion, thanks to Richard Carpenter's second-half blunderbuss of a shot. In the second leg at Withdean, Sam Parkin equalised with nine minutes left of the 90 minutes to force extra time, and on 97 minutes Rory Fallon put Swindon ahead. Albion looked to be on their way out of the play-offs, but with virtually the finally touch of the game, Adam Virgo headed Albion level to force a penalty shoot-out. Richard Carpenter, John Piercy, Chris Iwelumo and Virgo were all successful from the spot to give the Seagulls a 4-3 win; Albion keeper Ben Roberts saved from Swindon's Tommy Mooney, and Andy Gurney hit the post.

Club centenary

Albion turned 100 years old on 24 June 2001, and spent the whole year celebrating! From 1 January 2001, the team wore a special centenary kit, designed by chairman Dick Knight. On 18 May 2001 the club held a spectacular Centenary Evening of Legends at the Brighton Centre, hosted by TV presenters Des Lynam and Peter

Brackley. As the closest to Albion's first ever competitive fixture on 21 September 1901, the match with Bournemouth on 22 September 2001 was deemed the centenary match. Other events included a church service, Sussex Cricket Club veterans v an Albion XI cricket match at Henfield, and the play, Brighton 'Til I Die! The club also nominated 24 legends from its first 100 years. These were:

Charlie Webb	*Player and manager*	*1908-48*
Tommy Cook	*Player and manager*	*1921-29 and 1947*
Ernie Tug Wilson	*Player*	*1922-36*
Harry Baldwin	*Player*	*1939-52*
Johnny McNichol	*Player**	*1948-52*
Des Tennant	*Player*	*1948-59*
Glen Wilson	*Player and trainer†*	*1948-60 and 1962-86*
Eric Gill	*Player*	*1952-60*
Jimmy Langley	*Player*	*1953-57*
Bobby Smith	*Player*	*1964-65*
Norman Gall	*Player*	*1962-74*
Peter O'Sullivan	*Player*	*1970-81*
Brian Horton	*Player and manager*	*1976-81 and 1998-99*
Mark Lawrenson	*Player*	*1977-81*
Alan Mullery	*Manager*	*1976-81 and 1985-86*
Peter Ward	*Player*	*1975-80 and 1982-83*
Steve Foster	*Player*	*1979-84 and 1992-96*
Gary Stevens	*Player*	*1978-83*
Garry Nelson	*Player*	*1987-91*
Dean Wilkins	*Player and coach*	*1983-84, 1987-96 and 1998-*
Ian Chapman	*Player*	*1986-96*
Robbie Reinelt	*Player*	*1997-98*
Micky Adams	*Manager*	*1999-2001*
Bobby Zamora	*Player*	*2000-2003*

* Johnny McNichol was on the commercial staff at the club between 1979 and 1992.

† Glen Wilson was part of the backroom staff at the club as trainer, caretaker manager and kit man with the club until 1986.

Yes! Yes!

In 1999, Brighton & Hove City Council held a referendum asking the electorate two questions on the issue of a new stadium for Brighton &

Hove Albion. The first question was whether they supported the idea of a new stadium for the city's football club; the second was whether that stadium should be at the council-proposed site of Falmer, which was also favoured by the club. On 6 May 1999, Brighton & Hove awoke to 5,000 green and white balloons decorating the streets of the then-twin towns. The balloons were part of the YES YES campaign launched by the club's supporters, who had formed the Falmer For All group in support of the stadium bid. The aim was to urge locals to turn out and vote in favour of the new stadium. The electorate proved overwhelmingly in favour: 56,701 (83.5% of those voting) voted in favour of a permanent home for the Albion, and 44,985 (67.6%) voted in favour of the stadium being at Falmer.

Record transfer fee paid IV

Mark Lawrenson became the club's first six-figure purchase in June 1977, when the club paid the bizarre fee of £111,111 to Preston North End for the central defender's services. Alan Mullery outbid Liverpool, who were not prepared to pay over £100,000 for Lawrenson. It proved a canny piece of business, as the defender was quite possibly the finest player to appear for the club. He made 174 appearances and scored seven goals, before Liverpool paid nine times what they had originally been prepared to pay for the Eire international in August 1981. By that time, the record transfer fee paid by Albion had been broken four times:

Date	Player	Bought from	Fee
November 1977	Teddy Maybank	Fulham	£238,000
July 1979	John Gregory	Aston Villa	£250,000
June 1980	Gordon Smith	Glasgow Rangers	£400,000
June 1980	Michael Robinson	Manchester City	£400,000
October 1980	Andy Ritchie	Manchester United	£500,000

The half-a-million fee paid for Ritchie remains the club's biggest ever single purchase of a player; however, when Ritchie left for Leeds United in a straight-swap deal with Terry Connor in March 1983, the transfer was also rated at £500,000.

Back-to-back champions

Albion became only the seventh team in English football history to win back-to-back championships, when Peter Taylor led them to the Second Division title in 2001/02. A season earlier, under the guidance of Micky Adams, they had pipped Chesterfield to the Third Division title by five points – 14 if you count the nine-point deduction imposed on the Spireites for financial irregularities. Bobby Zamora's goals were a crucial factor. He managed 63 goals over the two seasons, and club captain Paul Rogers became the first man in the club's history to lift two championship trophies.

Football League Division Three 2000/01

Team	P	W	D	L	F	A	W	D	L	F	A	Points	GD
Albion	**46**	**19**	**2**	**2**	**52**	**14**	**9**	**6**	**8**	**21**	**21**	**92**	**+38**
Cardiff City	46	16	7	0	56	20	7	6	10	39	38	82	+37
Chesterfield	46	16	5	2	46	14	9	9	5	33	28	80	+37
Hartlepool United	46	12	8	3	40	23	9	6	8	31	31	77	+17
Leyton Orient	46	13	7	3	31	18	7	8	8	28	33	75	+8
Hull City	46	12	7	4	27	18	7	10	6	20	21	74	+8
Blackpool	46	14	4	5	50	26	8	2	13	24	32	72	+16
Rochdale	46	11	8	4	36	25	7	9	7	23	23	71	+11
Cheltenham Town	46	12	5	6	37	27	6	9	8	22	25	68	+7
Scunthorpe United	46	13	7	3	42	16	5	4	14	20	36	65	+10

Southend United	46	10	8	5	29	23	5	10	8	26	30	63	+2
Plymouth Argyl	46	13	5	5	33	17	2	8	13	21	44	58	-7
Mansfield Town	46	12	7	4	40	26	3	6	14	24	46	58	-8
Macclesfield Town	46	10	5	8	23	21	4	9	10	28	41	56	-11
Shrewsbury Town	46	12	5	6	30	26	3	5	15	19	39	55	-16
Kidderminster Harriers	46	10	6	7	29	27	3	8	12	18	34	53	-14
York City	46	9	6	8	23	26	4	7	12	19	37	52	-21
Lincoln City	46	9	9	5	36	28	3	6	14	22	38	51	-8
Exeter City	46	8	9	6	22	20	4	5	14	18	38	50	-18
Darlington	46	10	6	7	28	23	2	7	14	16	33	49	-12
Torquay United	46	8	9	6	30	29	4	4	15	22	48	49	-25
Carlisle United	46	8	8	7	26	26	3	7	13	16	39	48	-23
Halifax Town	46	7	6	10	33	32	5	5	13	21	36	47	-14
Barnet	46	9	8	6	44	29	3	1	19	23	52	45	-14

continued

Football League Division Two 2001/02

Team	P	W	D	L	F	A	W	D	L	F	A	Points	GD
Albion	**46**	**17**	**5**	**1**	**42**	**16**	**8**	**10**	**5**	**24**	**26**	**90**	**+24**
Reading	46	12	7	4	36	20	11	8	4	34	23	84	+27
Brentford	46	17	5	1	48	12	7	6	10	29	31	83	+34
Cardiff City	46	12	8	3	39	25	11	6	6	36	25	83	+25
Stoke City	46	16	4	3	43	12	7	7	9	24	28	80	+27
Huddersfield Town	46	13	7	3	35	19	8	8	7	30	28	78	+18
Bristol City	46	13	6	4	38	21	8	4	11	30	32	73	+15
QPR	46	11	10	2	35	18	8	4	11	25	31	71	+11
Oldham Athletic	46	14	6	3	47	27	4	10	9	30	38	70	+12
Wigan Athletic	46	9	6	8	36	23	7	10	6	30	28	64	+15
Wycombe Wanderers	46	13	5	5	38	26	4	8	11	20	38	64	-6
Tranmere Rovers	46	10	9	4	39	19	6	6	11	24	41	63	+3
Swindon Town	46	10	7	6	26	21	5	7	11	20	35	59	-10
Port Vale	46	11	6	6	35	24	5	4	14	16	38	58	-11
Colchester United	46	9	6	8	35	33	6	6	11	30	43	57	-11
Blackpool	46	8	9	6	39	31	6	5	12	27	38	56	-3
Peterborough United	46	11	5	7	46	26	4	5	14	18	33	55	+5
Chesterfield	46	9	3	11	35	36	4	10	9	18	29	52	-12
Notts County	46	8	7	8	28	29	5	4	14	31	42	50	-12

Northampton Town	46	9	4	10	30	33	5	3	15	24	46	49	-25
Bournemouth	46	9	4	10	36	33	1	10	12	20	38	44	-15
Bury	46	6	9	8	26	32	5	2	16	17	43	44	-32
Wrexham	46	7	7	9	29	32	4	3	16	27	57	43	-33
Cambridge	46	7	7	9	29	34	0	6	17	18	59	34	-46

Falmer plans

Albion first announced plans for a new 22,374-seat stadium at Falmer in March 1998. At that time, the club was in exile at Gillingham for home matches and fighting to return to a temporary home at Withdean. The planning application took over three years to prepare and was lodged with Brighton & Hove City Council in October 2001. The council approved the application by 11 votes to one in June 2002, but the application was then 'called in' by the Secretary of State and Deputy Prime Minister John Prescott. A first public inquiry was inconclusive and Prescott announced plans to re-open the inquiry. He finally gave the stadium the go-ahead on 31 October 2005. However, it has since been met with legal opposition by Lewes District Council, which is taking the matter to the High Court. As this book went to print, the club was still awaiting a final decision, despite the public support in the referendum (see 'Yes! Yes!', page 114), a successful planning application, two public inquiries and over 6000 letters to the Prime Minister, not to mention the thousands of letters and column inches supporting the project in the press. The graphic opposite shows an overview of the planned site at Falmer.

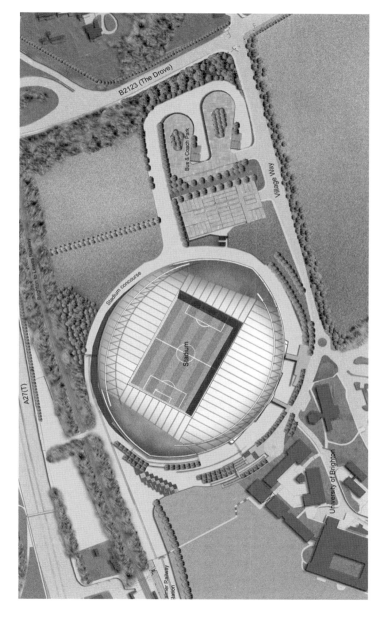

Bibliography

Albion A-Z: A Who's Who of Brighton & Hove Albion FC
Tim Carder and Roger Harris, Goldstone Books (1997)

Dicks Out - The Unique Guide to British Football Songs
Larry Bulmer and Rob Mills, Chatsby Publishing (1992)

England, Their England: The Definitive Story of Foreign Footballers in the English Game Since 1888
Nick Harris, Pitch Publishing (2003)

Seagulls! The Story Of Brighton & Hove Albion FC
Tim Carder and Roger Harris, Goldstone Books (1993)

Sunday Times Illustrated History Of Football
Chris Nawrat and Steve Hutchings, Ted Smart (1995)

Super Seagulls
John Vinicombe, George Nobbs Publishing (1980)

Up, Up, And Away
John Vinicombe, George Nobbs Publishing (1980)

Recommended websites

www.albionhistory.org.uk

www.clubsincrisis.com

www.thefa.com

www.thefootball-league.co.uk

www.northstandchat.biz

www.seagulls.co.uk

www.soccerbase.com

www.theargus.co.uk

www.wikipedia.org